The

8th

Day Of The Week

WHY IT DESTROYS BUSINESSES AND WHAT TO DO ABOUT IT

The 20 lessons you need to know now

George Bakrnchev, BBSc. (Psych.)

FOREWORD BY:

SONY VASANDANI, B.Com, M.Ed.

Published by Red Day® Coaching
Email: info@reddaycoaching.com
Website: www.reddaycoaching.com

Disclaimer
All the information, techniques, skills and concepts contained within this
publication are of the nature of general comment only, and are not in any way
recommended as individual advice. The intent is to offer a variety of information
to provide a wider range of choices now and in the future, recognising that we all
have widely diverse circumstances and viewpoints. Should any reader choose to
make use of the information contained herein, this is their decision, and the
contributors (and their companies), authors and publishers do not assume any
responsibilities whatsoever under any conditions or circumstances. It is
recommended that the reader obtain their own independent advice.
Any income statements and examples are not intended to represent or guarantee
that everyone will achieve the same results. Each individual's success will be
determined by his or her desire, dedication, effort, and motivation. There are no
guarantees you will duplicate the results stated here, recognising that any
business endeavour has inherent risk for loss of capital.

Red-Yellow-Green Days® and 24-170® are registered trademarks of Red Day®
Coaching

Ordering information
Quantity sales. Special pricing for quantity purchases of this book by
corporations, associations, and others is available. For details, please make
contact via email: info@reddaycoaching.com

What Others Are Saying
About The 8th Day Of The Week

'George makes you realise that what's been drummed into us for years simply doesn't work anymore, and reveals to us what we need to do to build a business that REALLY works. This book is a must read.'

Christopher Tolevsky CPA
Accountant & Business Development Specialist

'I have put George's theories into practice. The next time you find yourself distracted or procrastinating, read this quote from George's book: "From now on, every time you catch yourself doing a 10-cent activity ask yourself, 'What am I fearing that distracts me with 10-cent activities?' That will be your answer to what needs to be done to get to your next $100,000 level in your business.'"

Michelle Evans
Global Digital Media & Business Development Manager
4 Ingredients

'On the first day of working with George, my wife, Belinda, and I went home and applied Lesson 9. We saved $150K in costs. Since then we've innovated new products in record time, expanded our stores and have dramatically increased our family time.'

Mark Hobbs
Founder of Beefy's Pies

'George Bakrnchev is like a spiritual leader for business owners. In this book he delivers profound messages using simple examples that will revolutionise the way you view your business and your life.'

Nick Randall
Enlightened Owner of Golf Fit Pro

'What a great read! So true and so many business owners will relate to this book. I love the comparison to golf, very clever. It makes a great comparison between 'Ambition and Ability'. It's just what I needed to grow to the next level.'

Steve Hamilton
Managing Director - A.S.H Electrical

'After applying Lesson 8 in this book I have been getting amazing results, all brought about because of Red Days!'

Robert Biddle
Managing Director - Squeaky Clean

'This book challenges the conventional wisdom that working longer hours in a business equates to more success. George's lessons provide a framework for discovering a better way to build a bigger life. Our bottom line and our lives have been enriched by the mind-shifts we have made in the past three years.'

Brad Peters
Partner - Online Accounting and Taxation Solutions

'Amazing! Accurate! Articulate! Enlightening! Factual! Intuitive! Outstanding!
These are just a few of the words that hit me as I was reading your book.'

Trevor Gilliland
Caloundra Law, Business and Property Lawyers

'A definite must read for anyone in business who doesn't want to watch life pass them by whilst being a SLAVE to their business!'

Jahna Koehler
Freedom Super Services

'George's examples are the best, and the 24 hour concept is fantastic to make us understand the 'work less and make more of your life' mentality.'

Taty Hindes
Soul Space Graphic Design

'I can totally relate to Lesson 5 in the book. We were letting our team tell us how and when they wanted to work and, as business owners, we were working around this. Since changing the way we work, our team has become much happier and much more productive. Thanks to George and his highly knowledgeable coaching partners.'

Debbie Duncan
Partner - Online Accounting and Taxation Solutions

'George's message can truly change your life, if you let it. As a "far-right brainer" who lived the 8th day week life for too long, I can attest to how these principals and lessons can change a life.'

Tanya du Preez, CA
Finance Strategy Specialist and Broker - Loan Clinic

'The lucky ones find 'The 8th Day Of The Week' and embrace its wisdom. In it, they read about struggles and experiences which remind them of their own, and happily discover that a good life is made possible by consciously adopting principles that value working smarter rather than longer or harder.
If you are thinking of starting a business, read this book now. If you have started a business and are tired and dispirited, read this book now and revive that daring and imaginative person you used to be.'

Susan Moriarty
Human Rights Lawyer

Dedication

---

*To those who know there is a better way and
have the courage to seek it and apply it*

Contents

Foreword
By Sony Vasandani, B.Com. M.Ed.

'Beware The Shop Front', Lesson 1 from George's book, changed my life.

I have been in the field of early childhood education for the past 22 years. In 2006, I was running four preschools and a training centre in Jakarta and its neighbouring cities, and was also employed as a consultant to assist in revamping a preschool business in Auckland, New Zealand, whose owner wanted to be able to systemize and franchise it.

It was big stuff for me! With long hours of work and frequent flying, my life was filled with stress. I was mostly 'reacting' on a day-to-day basis to all that was happening with the schools, the training centre and the consulting.

On the outside, everything looked rosy. It was a great shop front.

On the inside, everything seemed out of my control and, irrespective of how I tried to organise myself, nothing worked.

I was in Perth in mid-2007, exploring yet another consultancy opportunity (yes, I didn't know how to say 'no' - everything was just a good opportunity), when I was invited to the Como Theatre for a screening of a business film.

That was the first time I heard George speak. The theatre was packed out with hundreds of people and yet I felt like he was only speaking to me. It felt like the movie he had produced and screened that evening, called 'The Big Lie' of owning a business, was made just for me to watch.

I had this immensely strong gut reaction that what I was doing in my business was out of sync with who I am and why I wanted to go into business in the first place. I felt both sick to the stomach and strangely excited about making changes.

George has that ability to make you feel as though everything you have done in the past has been an apprenticeship for a bigger future, that all the people who have helped you or wronged you in business were there as part of your lessons in growing.

From listening to George's story, I knew he had been in my shoes before - he knew what it was like to work yourself silly and constantly strive for more. I instantly signed on to be mentored by him.

I honestly did not know if I had the expendable income for this program, how I was going to reach Sydney from Indonesia the next month for the live mentoring, or how I was going to be able to take time off from all that I was doing. All I knew was that I had to be there.

You see, I am an extreme right-brained person and that was the first thing I found out – which was a big relief. Why? Because I forget and lose things, and take up a million projects, but am not able to follow through them.

Organising my life around George's activity system of Red, Yellow and Green Days® has worked wonders for me. The principles were simple to follow and easily applied. It took me eight 90-Day periods to get to where I wanted to be and live the life I wanted to – with more growth, more control and more free time than I had ever imagined.

George has shown me how to get out of the 8th Day Of The Week mentality and run two Jakarta based businesses successfully and look after my property portfolio, all while living my idyllic life on the Sunshine Coast, Australia.

I have seen the effect these lessons have had on many other business owners, but most importantly for me, I have witnessed first hand the effect it has on their families, and that's why I wish the same for you.

Free Download, Updates And Next Steps

<u>The 10 Mind Shifts Poster – Free Download</u>

To produce a different result, you need different thinking, a 'Mind Shift'.

I'd like to gift you the 10 Mind Shifts that we give to our clients to help remind them what to focus on on a daily basis so that they head towards 24-170® and away from working The 8th Day Of The Week.

Display it where you can see it on a daily basis as a reminder to apply what you have learned from this book.

Enter this link to download your poster:

www.reddaycoaching.com/poster

<u>Knowledge and Success Updates</u>

As a special thank you for investing in this book, I'd like to invite you to have special access to our knowledge and success updates that we share with our clients so that you too can continue to advance your business and your life.

Enter this link to receive your free updates and reports:

www.reddaycoaching.com/updates

How To Get Out Of The 8th Day Of The Week

There's an old saying:
'The teacher will appear when the student is ready'...

I have the 'teachers'. All you need to do now is let me know that the 'student' within you is ready to approach business in a different way.

If nothing changes, then nothing changes!

Give yourself the opportunity to work with us. We have affordable ways for you to do that. To find out more, simply connect with us by entering the following link:

www.reddaycoaching.com/start

Note To All Business Coaches, Life Coaches and Executive Coaches

If, after reading this book, you believe there is a match between the way we both see things, then I believe it's important for us to connect.

There are opportunities available for you to go deeper and to add-in the Red-Yellow-Green Day® and 24-170® trademarked strategies, highlighted in this book, to your existing business/life coaching model so that you can further enrich your clients' lives.

Simply enter this link to register your interest:

www.reddaycoaching.com/coaches

Introduction To The 8th Day Of The Week

'Work never stops,
people do!'

I was born into a hardworking family. The only thing my parents knew was work, and the only thing their parents knew was work.

My parents came from very poor farming villages in Eastern Europe and I often joke that my family was so poor that they could only afford to buy two vowels for their surname.

My father didn't have the luxury of finishing primary school. Work was valued more than learning. Work meant survival.

So when my parents arrived in Australia - the lucky country! - in their teens, the one thing they knew how to do was work. They had youth on their side, so they took advantage of it and literally worked seven days a week.

Work meant money, and money meant security, and security meant freedom.

What I've noticed as a business psychology specialist and as a business developer is that people don't need much of an excuse or reason to work hard. For my parents, it was escaping poverty and being able to secure a financially stable future for their kids.

When you look around and listen to all the advertising and marketing messages, you'll be bombarded with reasons to continue to work, not only hard, but harder and for longer, so you can have more.

I remember a moment in my life, when I was around 7 years of age, that has stuck with me ever since. I was standing in my backyard speaking with my dad. He was about to go to work again. It was a weekend and all I can remember is that I wished he'd stay home that day, so I asked him, 'Why don't you take a day off?'

His reply left me stunned!

'What would I do on a day off?'

As a kid, I could think of a million things to do, but my dad had been robbed of his youth and all he could think of doing was more work.

It is often said that we 'mirror' the habits of the people who have the most influence on us.

In my early years of business I mirrored my parents' work ethic.

Working hard is a habit and eventually that habit becomes your destiny.

In Australia the working week is 38 hours long for a full-time employee. I have had direct contact with and interviewed thousands of business owners, and on average they work over 60 hours a week. That's the same as working 8 days a week and most will suffer low profits and high stress.

If that's you, then you're an 8th day of the weeker, just like I was.

Up until my thirties, I'd been slogging my guts out 7 days a week with a very young family. Just like my parents did and their parents did as well.

And then it hit me.

Ankylosing Spondylitis.

A rare debilitating arthritic condition that causes inflammation and immense pain in your hips, back, neck and shoulder joints.

Getting out of bed for work was, at times, impossible. Lifting up my kids would be fraught with danger. On my worst days, I couldn't even lift my arm to brush my teeth, the pain was *that* sharp. Painkillers and anti-inflammatories were consumed on a daily basis like candy.

As a result my body felt numb, almost insensitive, almost dead. Yet as a business owner, I still had to get up and go to work.

When I look back at those dark days, I see that these obstacles were all opportunities in disguise.

> I made a decision, that if I couldn't work the normal long hours everyone else could, then I had to find a way to achieve the same results with half the effort.

This led me on a day by day, year by year, decade by decade journey of what activities would be essential for me to do and what activities I could eliminate from my daily routine, or at least teach someone else to do.

Because I literally couldn't work hard like everyone else, I was compelled to discover ways to work smarter.

The end result was that I made much more money than I ever did before, when I was working harder. I had more free time to look after my health and attend to all of my young kids' milestones.

This book will either give you the push you need to get out of business or the inspiration to get more into it in a new way. Whichever path you choose, it will be the right thing for you to do.

Before you decide if you should be reading this book, let me be totally upfront with you about what I believe to be true about owning and running a business:

I want to share with you why this book is so close to my heart.

I want to share with you what I believe.

I believe that owning a business is one of the riskiest, craziest, dumbest things you can ever do in your lifetime!

Owning a business will rob you financially, it will rob you emotionally, it will rob you physically and, eventually, it will rob your spirit.

If you knew what it really meant to go into business, you would leave your money in the bank and go and work for somebody else.

But what I also know to be true is that business ownership can also become one of your life's greatest achievements.

The fact you are reading this right now means to me that you have stopped working for a few minutes to see if there is a better way.

There is! But you will need to stop working for a few more minutes to read the lessons in this book on how to work smarter not harder so that you can truly increase the value of your business and your life before it's too late.

Work never stops, people do!

With that in mind I wish for you not only a bigger bank balance, but also a bigger balance in all areas of your life.

These lessons are not just for this generation, but for all future generations to come.

You will see that they are timeless, and it is your time now to master them and pass them on to others who you value.

To your life.

George

P.S. To receive even more value from this book, please see the contents section titled 'Free Download, Updates And Next Steps' on how you can do that.

Lesson 1: Beware The Shop Front

'Despite the happy talk, the shop front, most business owners work the equivalent of eight days a week.'

I use to be an 8th day of the week business owner.

My business consumed me like a piranha and body rolled me like a croc.

Some days, I didn't even know if it was a Sunday or a Wednesday.

You might think that not being busy is worse than being busy, but let me tell you: it's not!

Being too busy is worse. Being busy doesn't mean you are making money, it just means you are busy. And if you are not making enough profit, then you are simply not making enough profit on a busier scale.

When you become an 8th day of the weeker, you lose yourself physically, emotionally, financially, spiritually and relationally. You become lost in a world of make-believe.

You believe that, by working harder, you can make all of your money worries disappear. You can't!

You believe that skipping meals will make you achieve more. It doesn't.

You believe that doing things yourself, rather than employing others, will save you money. It may do in the short term, but the reality is you will end up being the loser.

You believe that being away from your family and friends is only a short-term fix. It isn't. It becomes your daily habit and in the end you become a stranger to those you love.

As a business psychology specialist, people open up to me.

Often I am the first person a business owner sits down with and tells about their life, about their business, and about their relationships - not the 'Shop Front' version they give to others, but as it really is for themselves.

It is a great honour to be the person that people confide in. I know how difficult and yet liberating it can be to 'fess up' and tell it as it is.

What I've discovered over the years is that we business owners are great at 'Happy Talking'. We're an optimistic bunch. We have to be otherwise we would never have the guts to get into or stay in business in the first place.

We constantly 'Happy Talk' ourselves into a little place called 'Rosyland'.

'Rosyland' is great, but it doesn't pay the bills or keep our relationships in tact.

Next time you go to a business function, listen in to the answers business people give to the all-famous question: 'How's business?' This is when you really hear 'Happy Talk' in action.

'Happy Talk' sounds a little like this: 'Good, good,' 'Yeah, good, loving it!' 'Couldn't be better.' 'We're getting there!'

I am sure you've heard much better ones yourself, but I can tell you from speaking to business owners heart-to-heart from all over the globe that what they have been telling everyone is mostly a huge shop front - a cover up - which is concealing a much darker reality.

Their response is not meant to mislead you - it's actually meant to remind themselves that they should keep going. That all of their blood, sweat and tears will be all worth it one day.

REALITY CHECK: For those of us who take the grand leap of faith to go into business a full 96% of us will fail. If 100 businesses started today only 20 of them will be around in 5 years. And only 4 of those remaining 20 will be around in the next 5 years. Happy Talk only leads to low profits, high stress and eventually no business and a wasted life.

Sure we hear of super successful small businesses and how the owners struggled and beat all odds to become squillionaires, just like we hear about the gambler who went to the casino and won the jackpot, but how much did he lose and give up before he won the jackpot?

Despite the happy talk, the shop front, most business owners work the equivalent of eight days a week.

How do you know if you qualify for admittance into the 8th day of the week club?

Simple: Write down what time you would normally start and finish each day in a typical working week.

That's one figure... now, for the second figure:

Calculate the hours you spend 'talking' and 'brainstorming' about your business with your partner or spouse outside of your normal working hours. Don't kid yourself, these are working hours too.

Now add those hours to the first figure.

If your first figure is on average over sixty hours a week, then welcome to the 8th day of the week club. You have gained priority entry,

If your first and second figures combined exceed sixty hours then you too have gained entry into the 8th day of the week club.

If the combined figures exceed seventy-five hours a week, then you have top priority entry - go to the top of the queue!

(I'm not sure what you're queuing up for but I can tell you it's not worth it.)

If you have worked out that you have met the criteria for entry to the 8th day of the week club, don't think it's an exclusive club. It's not. It's littered with perfectionists, escapists and control freaks.

I use to be there, but I gave up my membership many years ago.

Here is what I can tell you about the 8th day of the week club: Owning and working an 8th day of the week business will rob you financially, it will rob you emotionally, it will rob you physically and eventually it will rob your desire.

You're most likely familiar with the saying 'work smarter not harder'. For many years I struggled to find anyone who could define what that really meant, especially for a workaholic business owner like me.

I made it my mission to discover not only what work smarter not harder really meant but also if it was possible to create a simple formula to help guide us business owners.

In my quest I literally locked myself away for five days in a seaside town called Noosa on the Sunshine Coast, Australia.

During those five days I reflected on what I had been able to achieve in my business keeping in mind that due to my debilitating arthritic condition I could only work limited hours.

There was a pattern.

I reflected back on the many changes I had made in my life and the dramatic improvements in my health and in the profits of my business.

My business was earning over $50,000 a month and I was working less than 24 hours a week as a business trainer and consultant. I had no desk and my profits were increasing every year. I had a small administration team to take care of things that I either wasn't good at or simply didn't enjoy doing and on top of that I was taking over 170 days off a year.

From this reflection, I created and trademarked the world's first formula for working smarter not harder called 24-170®. I swapped the Monday to Sunday system for Red-Yellow-Green Days® (more about that in the next lesson).

I've invested over a decade of my life working with small business owners and helping them apply the strategies behind 24-170®. My business got to the point where I needed other coaches and trainers to join me in helping other business owners apply 24-170® to their business.

My first franchise partners came from my existing clients who had benefited so much from the strategies that they had freed themselves enough out of their businesses to be able to take on a partnership role within my company.

Together we are all helping business owners re-write the rulebooks on how business and life gets done.

I invite you to make 24-170® a part of your ongoing business strategy, for it has many riches, both financially and personally.

To help you get started I want you to imagine that your business is a ball game.

No ball game is played without an end goal. A goal post or target if you like, just as in golf.

If we accept that your business can be viewed as a game, then what are the target posts for this game called business?

If there were no target posts in golf, who would go and watch it? Who would join up and play it? It would just become a mad run around the field with no purpose and a lot of very busy aimless people.

Sadly, this is how most people play the game of business.

Here is how many others and I play the game of business. 24-170® has four clearly defined target posts to aim at.

Here they are:

Imagine if you re-structured your business so that:

1/ You work a MAXIMUM of 24 hours a week
2/ You take a MINIMUM of 170 days off a year
3/ You have no desk for yourself as the owner of the business
4/ You have increasing yearly profits

Now ask yourself, if your business was set up in this way, how much more valuable would your business and your personal life be?

Let's begin by bridging the gap between where you are right now and where you want to be in relation to those 4 target posts.

Time for you to be proactive now and fill in the missing gaps.

Once you know what the gaps are, you'll be on your way to creating a highly valuable business and life.

The Goal: 24-170®	Your Current Status	The Gap – The New Goal
1/ Work a MAX of 24hrs/week	I work _____ hours/week	Decrease my hours worked per week by _____
2/ Take a MIN of 170 days off/year	I take _____ days off per year	Increase my days off by _____ per year
3/ Have No Desk	I have (circle) 0, 1, 2, 3+ Desks	Decrease my number of desks by _____
4/ Have Increasing Yearly Profits	I have (circle) increasing / decreasing / similar yearly profits	Increase my yearly profits by _____

Now, lets bridge the gap together lesson by lesson…

Lesson 2: Get Rid Of The Monday To Sunday System

> *'Employees work in the*
> *TIME = MONEY economy.*
> *You don't!'*

The way you get paid, as a business owner, is entirely different to how an employee gets paid.

If you don't know the difference, you will be destined for a lifetime of low profits and high stress.

Business owners get paid for the *results* they produce. Employees get paid for the *time* they put in.

This is what I mean:

As a business owner, if you work 10 hours you will only get paid if your 10 hours of input produces a result. If it doesn't, you simply don't get paid.

As an employee if you work 10 hours, you will get paid for the 10 hours of input irrespective of the result it produces.

Lets take a pie making business as an example. I don't have to know how to make a pie, nor do you, in order to own a pie shop. We can get others to do that work. This frees us up to focus on growing the business.

> **NOTE:** If we did know how to make pies, we probably wouldn't have any time left to focus on growing the business. So the wisdom here (if you haven't got a business yet), is to get into a business where you don't have the technical know how, so that you don't get sucked into doing the

technical work of the business. This way you will be free to focus on the strategic work, which is what is needed in order to seriously grow a business - any business.

On the other hand, if you own a business and you have already been well and truly sucked into doing the technical work of your business, then read on carefully as I have your 'exit' strategy detailed in the new work system below.

Now, back to the pie making business...

We pay the pie maker for the number of hours they work.

Employees work in the TIME = MONEY economy. You don't!

When an employee works 10 hours, they get paid for 10 hours. They do overtime, they get paid overtime.

When you really think about it, being an employee is a highly profitable business model. Apart from minimal travel/food/clothing expenses, almost all of their net income is pure profit.

Often an employee makes more money than a business owner and, on top of this, there is little to no risk for the employee.

An employee doesn't have to mortgage their home, give personal guarantees, or have an overdraft. They are entitled to superannuation, sick leave, holiday pay, every weekend off for life...it's almost the perfect, little business.

What about us, the business owners?

Well, we get paid for the results we produce from our business at the end of each day.

We work in the RESULTS = MONEY economy.
If there is a good financial result, we make money, if there is a poor result, we lose money. If there is a break even result, we break even too.

Business ownership is the highest risk business model you can think of. There are no guarantees, we may have to sign over everything we own to a lender to get into or to grow the business. We can work 24 hours a day, 7 days a week and there is no law against it. We don't have to save any money in our superannuation, we don't have holiday pay or sick leave and we don't get paid for public holidays. It's all on us and it's all up to us!

Our business success is not dependant on how many hours we put in, but by what results we produce. That's both a blessing and a curse.

I'm going to help you make it a blessing.

I have NEVER worked as a full-time employee in my entire life. You could say that I'm not employable. I would just want to change everything in the other person's business. I wouldn't be able to help myself, because I know there would be a better way of doing it. As a result, I've always owned my own business and I have never had financial stability. I've always worked for a result and I wouldn't have it any other way.

So, as entrepreneurs, you and I work in the Results = Money economy.

If you're a commission sales person, then be mindful that you fall under the system of a business owner and not an employee. You ultimately get rewarded for the results you produce, not for the amount of hours you put in.

The Monday to Sunday system works perfectly for employees, who get paid for their time. It's easy to use the Monday to Sunday system to pay employees as all we need to know is what days they worked and how many hours they put in.

But this system doesn't work for business owners like you and I. We don't get paid for our time. It doesn't matter if we are working on a Monday, a Thursday or a Sunday. All that matters is what result did our business produce for the day? The Week? The Month? The Quarter? The Year?

So if it doesn't matter what day of the week it is, then what does matter for a business owner?

The number one thing that matters most for our results is what ACTIVITIES DID WE DO on any given day?

We know that when we do certain types of activities, we get certain types of results.

It has been well documented that, when business owners work ON the business, they grow and prosper. There is no limit to how far the business can grow.

When business owners work IN the business they get results limited to the number of hours the business owner can put in. The business will never grow beyond a certain level.

A business owner's results are driven by the TYPE of ACTIVITIES we do, NOT by the number of hours or days we put into the business.

We need to swap the Monday to Sunday System
for the Red – Yellow – Green Day® System

The Monday to Sunday system was not built for business owners.

We need a system that focuses on better results, not on putting in more time.

I noticed that all of the results for a business owner are a consequence of the type of activities they do or don't do.

It's why I designed a three colour activity system that a business owner needs to use to boost their results:

They are: **Red – Yellow – Green Day**® Activities.

Red Day® Activities = Working ON the business (finding ways to sell more pies)

Yellow Day® Activities = Working IN the business (making the pies) and

Green Day™ Activities = NO work whatsoever (100% non-business activities)

Most business owners still operate as if they are employees in the time = money system. It's why most businesses fail and will continue to fail irrespective of how hard they work.

It's why most business owners fall prey to the 8th Day Of The Week syndrome.

Replace the Monday to Sunday System for Red – Yellow – Green Days® and watch your results magnify!

Red Days® are the days where you do strategic thinking and strategic work, where you work ON the business.

On a Red Day® you find ways to make the business better. You create/modify products or services for your customers. You create/modify systems for your business so that it can look, feel, sound and taste better to your customers, your employees, your suppliers and your lenders. You look at finding ways to get your customers to come back more often, get them to spend more with you (ethically), get them to refer to you, and get feedback from your top customers. It's a relationship building day because relationships also equal money. This is all Red Day® work.

Yellow Days® are the days where you do the technical work of your business, where you work IN the business.

On a Yellow Day® you serve customers, you do the accounts, you open the business, close the business, you employ people, you order stock, you follow up on orders, and you check the quality of the work that goes out. It's the 'stuff' of your business. This is all Yellow Day® work.

If you're a business owner and all you get to do is yellow Day® work, then all you are doing is 'stuff', and if all you do is stuff, then all you'll have at the end is 'stuff all'. Harsh, I know, but I see it everyday and I am hell bent on changing that for you.

Green Days™ are the days where you do NO business.

Green Days™ means no business emails, no business reading, no business talking, no business thinking. So, what do you do on a Green Day™? Anything and everything that is not related to business. And yes, it's the hardest day for a business owner to take, because they are so conditioned to work they wouldn't know what to do on a Green Day™.

If it helps, let me share with you that I know exactly what that is like. In the early years of my working life I never took Green Days™. When I first attempted to, I almost felt sick with worry and guilt that I wasn't working. It was as if everything was going to collapse or I was going to miss out on opportunities to make my business grow.

I look back now and it's the complete opposite. I cannot imagine working on a Green Day™. I've become so accustomed to resting, rejuvenating, playing golf and catching up with friends on a Green Day™, that to think of working on a Green Day™ makes me feel guilty.

You can have half a Red Day® or half a Yellow Day®, but you can't have half a Green Day™. With Green Days™ it's all or nothing.

I have achieved so much more as a result of changing to this system and I cannot begin to tell you how much better off my clients and I are. It's a total win-win. Your business grows, your health grows, and you grow.

Remember: You get paid for your results, not your time. The Red-Yellow-Green Day® system is a results based system. Make it so for you too.

Lesson 3: Time Management Is A Myth

'The 8th Day Of The Week Buster:
Manage Your Activities Not Your Time!'

An 8th day of the week business owner believes that they can manage their time…

Peter, a retail store owner, came up to me after a business seminar and told me very openly that he was fed up with his business, fed up with his never ending struggle to keep family commitments and fed up with his demanding clients. He told me that there just wasn't enough time to do what needed to be done!

He was a bit taken a back when I agreed that he was 100% correct - 'there simply isn't enough time to do what needs to be done.'

Without giving him an 8th day of the week solution, I asked what he thought the solution might be?

He replied, 'Time management… I just have to learn how to manage my time better… I'm just not good at managing my time.'

I told Peter that his answer was very typical of an 8th day of the week worker. I asked him, 'Do you believe that you have to work hard to get ahead? And, if so, do you believe that you have to manage your time better?'
'Yes, yes, that's it!' he said.

I stared straight at him and said, 'You're 100% wrong Peter. It's NOT!' (I was overly forceful but I wanted to see how glued he was to his idea of time management).

I explained to Peter that to manage something is to make it faster, slower, heavier, lighter etc. You can manage your money - you can make it grow, you can even make it shrink, but you can't do the same with time.

'Your resource called time is NOT manageable Peter and I'm going to prove it to you in less than 5 seconds!'

'I want you to look at your wrist watch very fiercely and, for the next 5 seconds, I want you to manage your time by speeding up those 5 seconds, by slowing down those 5 seconds and, if you can, I want you to make time stop altogether.'

All Peter could do in 5 seconds was watch those 5 seconds go by.

We all fail at time management because time is not manageable!

The ONLY thing Peter could have done in those 5 seconds is manage what ACTIVITY he did in those 5 seconds.

He could have danced for 5 seconds. He could have screamed for 5 seconds. He could have fired someone in 5 seconds. He could have created a solution in 5 seconds. He could do what ever he wanted to do, but he could not make 5 seconds any longer or shorter than 5 seconds.

As a business developer, you have to know what activities you MUST be doing and what activities you must NEVER be doing.

There are 3 types of activity that all business developers must be aware of in order to break free of the 8th day of the week syndrome. You'll discover what they are for you in the next lesson.

Lesson 4: There Are Only 3 Types Of Activities In Your Day

'What you don't see,
you don't value.'

From the previous lesson, you now know that your time is not manageable, but your activities are.

When you become aware that there are only 3 types of activities in a business owner's life, you will be able to see clearly that doing the wrong ones will suffocate your business and your life. And, by the same token, you will see that, by doing the right activities, you will catapult your business and your sanity to a completely new level.

Sandie came to me with one of the busiest schedules I have ever seen for a business owner and on top of that she had a husband, two kids and a mother-in-law to look after. She owned 4 pre-school centres. Every day of the week involved work.

On Sundays she did her 'quiet time work' as there were no work interruptions on that day. Without knowing it at the time, she was putting in over eighty hours per week. She had bought into the classic 8th day of the week work harder mantra.

I asked her how she felt about herself and her business right now:

> She answered bravely, 'I am frazzled! Everyone wants
> a piece of me and I spend my days reacting to
> whatever gets thrown at me. I've lost my passion for
> what I do. I just want to throw it all away and
> disappear.'

Sandie's response was the same response that I have heard over and over again. She thought that her crazy schedule was typical of the industry she was in. She said that, in the education field, everyone demands so much of you. 'My teachers, my pupils, my management team, they all wanted my attention every day.'

At least that was the 'story' she was convincing herself with. When I explained to her that her story was the same story I had heard the day before from a retailer, from a manufacturer and from an accountant, only then did she realise that it wasn't an industry problem.

It was a human problem.

She just takes on too much and wants to please everyone.

Before I offered to help her I asked her my number one pre-help question:

Are you coachable?

She answered with a sigh, 'Yes, I am coachable. I'm sick and tired of trying to be a super woman who believes that asking for advice or mentoring is a sign of weakness.'

I then told her in the language she would understand best that 'the right teacher' would appear when 'the student' is ready. Sandie smiled widely and said she was ready.

I promptly handed her a sheet to fill in for the next seven days. It had three columns on it.

The first column was the time of day, the second column was the type of activity she was doing and the third column was a question:

'Would your customers care if YOU did this activity or not: Yes or No?'

Meaning: If someone else did that activity, ultimately would it make any difference to your customers?

In this type of business, Sandie's customers were the parents, not the students. The parents ultimately decided if their kids went to her pre-school or someone else's.

For the next 7 days Sandie was asked to write down every activity she did. It included business actions and non-business actions, like cooking, shopping, picking up kids etc. I wanted ALL of her weekly activities written down.

This is a very powerful process.

What I love about it is that it makes the invisible VISIBLE.

What you don't see, you don't value.

For the first time in nineteen years of business, Sandie could actually see what type of work she really spends her time doing on a daily basis. This was the raw material I needed in order to show her how to bust out of the 8th day of the week trap.

I looked over her activities for the week and told her that they would fall into three Activity Zones and that we have to get rid of two of the zones from her life for good!

She was feeling excited and apprehensive (that's always a good sign. It means people are wanting to change, but they don't know how to do it. The 'how' will come).

Here are the three activity Zones and Sandie's results for each:

Zone 1: The 'NO-GO' Zone

- It's stuff you're NOT capable of doing. For Sandie it was activities like trying to fix the intricate computer network at her school.
- Zone 1 activities are an insult to your capabilities.
- If time or money was no option, you would delegate this work NOW.
- They are huge confidence and energy zappers.
- You end up taking lousy Red, Yellow and Green Days®.

Sandie Spent 3% of her time in this zone

Zone 2: The 'I'll Handle It' Zone

- You hear yourself saying, '*It's ok...I'll handle it*'. For Sandie it was organizing the teaching rosters, and it consumed a lot of her time and mental energy.
- You know what has to be done, but you end up doing it.
- You're very competent at it, but you're NOT unique at it.
- You say you don't have the time or money to teach anyone else to do it.
- You can see where you should be investing your time, but you're not.
- You end up taking lousy Red, Yellow and Green Days®.

Sandie Spent 93% of her time in this zone

Zone 3: The 'Unique Talent' Zone

- It's your natural ability. For Sandie it was creating new and exciting programmes that set her schools apart from all others in her country.
- In this zone, your energy and confidence level is always up.
- Your creativity levels are at their highest.
- You get highly excited doing what you do here.
- You take highly productive Red, Yellow and Green Days®.

For clients who can't figure out what their Unique Talent is, I ask them this one question (and you can't answer by saying: banking the money):

> **If I could get everything handled in your business by a team of professionals, except for one thing, what is the 'one thing' that you would love to keep doing in your business, day in, day out?**

Sandie Spent 4% of her time in this zone

So with this realisation, I showed Sandie what her year would look like if she didn't change anything:

In Zone 1 (No Go)	In Zone 2 (I'll Handle It)	In Zone 3 (Unique Talent)
3%	93%	4%

I sat her down and said to her in plain English, 'If you don't change this, you will be destined for a life of low profits and high stress!'

Once we made the invisible, visible, the next step was pretty clear. Sandie had to start the process of eliminating ALL Zone 1 and 2 activities.

> **You will find that highly successful and balanced business owners are working in their Zone 3 activities at least 80% of the time!**

Zone 1 and 2 activities are 'stuff' items and if all you consume your day with are 'stuff' items then all you will be left with is 'stuff all' (Australian slang for 'Nothing').

Sandie was out of balance and lacked energy and passion because over time, as she grew her business, she allowed herself to get trapped into doing low level Zone 1 and 2 activities - stuff that she was not unique at.

Only 4% of her time was invested in doing activities she was unique at.

It's like landing a job with a company and they get you to work 96% of your time doing activities that bored and frustrated you. How long would you stay? How much money would they have to pay you to make you stay?

I also use the Zone 1, 2, 3 system to help business owners recruit the right employees. They focus now on employing people with Zone 3 skills. You don't want to employ a Zone 2 bookkeeper who can handle the books but is not unique at it.

You will want to build a business where Zone 3 talent surrounds you, where everyone is employed to do what he or she is unique at. Moaning and groaning employees are usually the ones that are employed to do work they are not unique at. They'll complain about their working conditions, their pay and their fellow workers, in fact anything and everything, because they simply don't like doing what they are doing. It's not their ZONE.

I also use the Zone 1, 2, 3 system to build a great sales system, which is aimed at increasing sales. And I mean REALLY increasing sales.

Imagine you employ a sales person to sell your product or service, and selling is a Zone 3 activity (unique talent) for this person. All they want to do is to be left alone to sell - they love winning new business.

Anyone who loves to sell will tell you that they hate doing the activity that follows when making the sale (Zone 2 for them – the

'I'll handle it' Zone). The dreaded paperwork, phone calls, scheduling of the next steps... in fact any activity that takes them away from winning new business is a drain on their energy and their love of selling.

As a business developer you have to ask yourself, 'How can I get them to keep selling at least 80% of the time, without doing non-selling - Zone 2 - activities?'

Solve this and you will have a selling machine that loves selling and follow up employees that love to do the follow up, because it's their Zone 3 to do that type of activity.

Now you can see why time management is useless. Asking a sales person to manage their time better by doing Zone 2 work won't solve the fundamental issue – they hate doing the follow up. It's not their Zone, so why hit your head against the wall trying to get them to manage their time better?

They won't manage their time better. FULL STOP. Time is NOT manageable, but what they will happily do is manage the activities they love to do better.

Applying the Zone 1, 2, 3 system in your business can eliminate so much business stress. The best time to do this is the day you start your business, even if you're the only one in the whole company. Grow with this strategy in mind and your business will grow with you in a Zone 3 way.

I did this with my business development and coaching business. At the very start I was the only employee, and over time I brought people in one by one and all of us did solely Zone 3 work. The only time my business and my personal life suffered was when I took on people that were asked to do activities they were not unique at.

Most businesses will fail because they have allowed themselves to be trapped in doing work they simply do not enjoy and are not unique at.

Business failure has got nothing to do with the economy or the competition. Zone 3 people always overcome these obstacles.

Back to Sandie, the activities she loved to do and the reason she went into business in the first place was that she knew she could do it better than what was on offer at the time. She knew she had a better way of educating preschoolers in her country.

NOTE TO SELF: Nowhere does it say that, as a business owner, I have to do activities that I hate doing. From now on I am ONLY going to do Zone 3 activities and I'm going to delegate or eliminate the rest.

Lesson 5: Don't Pay People To Stress You Out!

'Free up their future' - let them go and play someone else's game.

Billy was in the removals business. Within two years of meeting and working with Billy and his wife, they went on and built a fleet of trucks from very humble beginnings. Their business journey fascinated me.

At the start, business and life was pretty simple; it was just Billy and a truck. Expenses were low and easy to see and manage - you know the sort of things, some small ads in the paper, petrol for the week, mobile phone bill, lease on a truck. Not much else to worry about except finding the next job.

I remember Billy very well. He was one of those seminar attendees that come in late. I remember he entered quietly, but as the speaker at the front I couldn't escape seeing him walk in.

Once I had finished speaking that evening, Billy was one of the first people to come up to me to say, 'Hi'. He apologized for coming in late, (8th day of the week people apologise a lot!) and proceeded to explain that he was the whole business, just him and a truck, and a labourer. He said he knew where he wanted to take his business, but there just weren't enough hours in the day to get there.

He was literally a one-man business, working the classic 8th day of the week and more. He was tired and frustrated, yet excited and confident about the future.

He told me something very profound - something that I don't normally hear from business owners very early on in their careers:

He said that he knew how to move people's possessions, but he didn't know how to build a business that moved people's possessions!

That was genius! When he said that to me I told him not to worry, that acknowledging and knowing the difference between the two destined him for bigger things in life.

And bigger things did come.

Billy's wife had left a full time, secure and well paid job to take over the office work of their business. I didn't tell them at the time, but it really is a bold move leaving a secure job and I admired them greatly for doing it.

> For me it's no big deal to leave a secure job, because I never had one. I've been self-employed all of my life. I'm basically unemployable and I wouldn't have it any other way.

I love business owners purely because they have enormous belief in the future - they draw great strength and courage from what may happen tomorrow.

I knew that what they were doing would pay dividends for them, but I wasn't sure if they had the same level of confidence in themselves as I did.

Most people can't do what Billy and his wife, Michelle did as it puts way too much stress on a marriage, but some can do it and they learn to do it very well.

Michelle went on to handle most of Billy's Zone 1 and 2 activities. This was a huge relief for Billy. He was now free to do what he loved to do best: meet new prospects and convert them into new clients.

The business boomed! Before they knew it, they had six removal trucks and a team of twelve employees.

Every ninety days they were breaking records - bigger average dollar sales, bigger referrals, fewer breakages, quicker turnaround times, higher up sells and cross sells, and higher net profits.

With any business that grows so fast, there is a tendency to take your eyes off the ball. They had employed people faster than they could have imagined. Even though they had a good hiring system, they told me that, at times, they felt like the only recruitment question they were asking was, 'Can you start today?'

> The day you decide to grow your
> business is also the day you decide to
> increase the complexities in your life.

The biggest complexities in your life will be people - not machines or systems, but people. The more you have, the more you will need to look after.

Billy was coming to me with different problems now. In the early days, it was about growing the business, getting more clients, and getting them to spend more ethically. Now it was all about people problems.

He showed me his monthly salaries bill to impress upon me how big his issues were. He shared with me how stressful running the business had become due to having so many different personalities in the team, and how some of them threatened the very existence of the business. He was totally stressed out by it all.

And that's when it hit me: Billy was paying people to stress him out!

What an absurd idea. Imagine paying people to stress you out! Who in their right mind would do that? It never starts that way, of course. It just ends up that way, UNLESS you do something to change it. I asked Billy if he agreed that paying people to stress him out was a stupid idea. Luckily he agreed. I suggested that we apply some of my Reverse Thinking™ strategies.

I asked him to 'reverse' the negative into a positive.

Instead of paying people to stress us out, we reversed it to, 'Paying people to remove our stress.'

Out of this grew his businesses motto: 'The stress free movers'.

Who wouldn't want to move home or office with a company that guarantees a stress free move, right? But - and it is a big BUT - for his business to live up to its motto, the people behind the motto had to be living the stress-free culture too.

This is was no easy task. Business is a lot like family, everyone wants perfect harmonious relationships within the family, but it's not always possible. The difference in business is that you get to lay down the rules of the game and what is acceptable and what isn't.

Don't pay people to stress you out. If people are not coachable, don't waste your or their time. People who are not happy in an environment end up getting sick or at least will make others sick. You owe it to them to help them lead a more fuller and richer life.

'Free up their future' - let them go and play someone else's game.

They'll thank you for it later once all the dust has settled and you won't have to work the 8th day of the week in order to pick up all of the work that hasn't been done.

Lesson 6: Business Is Only A Game!

'Your business is a game.
It's not life or death'.

Have you ever had to change a car tyre?

What about a truck tyre?

It's tough work, and it's even tougher if you have to run a business that changes tyres.

I'd just finished explaining to a group of business owners that everything I had just taught them could be applied to any business, when a big burly bloke came up to me and said, 'This stuff wouldn't work on my business'.

Instead of defending my position, I asked him why he thought that was the case.

He explained, with a fair bit of enthusiasm, that his business wasn't a dainty office type business, that his business didn't attract college graduates, that his people only worked for money, and that it was impossible to get a group of burly men to work as a team.

I could see right away that Paul was frustrated, yet looking for a solution at the same time. I knew he was ready to give something new a go, but it had to fit in with his character and with his employees' character.

So I asked Paul if he enjoyed playing or watching any sports. He laughed and said, 'C'mon. Look at me! Do I look like someone who plays sports? But I do love rugby league footy.'

For the next three or four minutes we forgot about business and only spoke about the game he loves. He spoke with so much passion: his energy levels immediately lifted, his body language became more animated, and his enthusiasm lit up his eyes and face.

I asked him if he had noticed any difference in himself when he spoke about the game he loves and when he spoke about his business.

He said, 'Yeah, my business sucks and it's draining me. That's why I've got no energy for it.'

I asked him point blank, 'Paul, do you want to know what the problem is?'

'Tell me.' he said. 'YOU!' I told him.

'You are the problem and you are the solution. When your footy team is not doing well who do we blame? The coach, right? And in your business you are the coach.'

I then asked him to put on his coach's cap and to look at his business like a game. 'Now tell me in a flash Paul, what is wrong with your team?'

He fired back, 'I think I have the wrong men in the wrong positions. We all think we are running a business, but in reality we are running a game of business. And it's up to me as the coach to identify who should be playing what position.

My team needs to see that everyone has a unique role to play and that each role affects the next player's role, which affects the scoreboard!'

He looked at me with this, 'Damn it, I think I've got it' type of look. It's the look I love to see in every business owner's face.

He said I'm going to sit down tonight and work out my team's structure and tomorrow I'm going to go in and let everyone know what position is available. If they want to fit into that position, great. If they don't, then that's great too as I'll get a chance to re-hire a passionate player for that specific position.

True to his word, Paul went in the next morning all fired up.

He shared his love for the game of footy and explained that no great footy team operates without a coach and expert players.

He told them that he wanted to recruit and develop a championship team. One that would win the industry's major award - the best of the best in the tyre industry - within the next twelve months.

Paul adapted to the 'my business is a game' model, broke down the business into four quarters and focused all results around a projected and actual scoreboard - just as you would in a game of footy.

By the end of the four quarters, Paul and his team had beaten 210 other tyre businesses to be crowned number one!

He did the impossible. Paul saw his business as a game. He transformed his business from a rowdy group of individuals into a championship team. So can you.

Lesson 7: The 24-Hour Human Battery

'The 24-hour human battery exists in all business owners. It just hasn't been turned on in the right way'.

The biggest failing of business owners is that they have huge amounts of energy. At least, it's like that when they first start out in business.

I can assure you, business has a way of knocking that youthful energy out of you very quickly.

I see many business owners getting through the 8th day of the week mentality by telling themselves that things will eventually get better.

They invariably don't.

Once a business gets established, surviving the first five years, business owners quickly and easily justify the 8th day of the week mentality by telling themselves that it will eventually build more profits!

They have to tell themselves this because it has to compensate in their mind for the crazy long hours they put in, the lack of family time, the physical neglect of themselves and the emotional neglect of their loved ones.

Your business is there to create a bigger life for you and your loved ones. It's not there to take the life you have away from you.

Please get that and get that fast!

Bevan and Julie came to me after initially working with me a decade ago. During that time they went on and developed a highly successful and industry-awarded chain of food stores. All stores were open seven days a week.

What impressed me the most about them was their respect and love for each other and their kids, despite becoming trapped by the 8th day of the week mentality. This is rare - once couples start working crazy hours their relationship invariably starts to deteriorate fast.

Julie was the relationship glue and she wasn't going to let a business take away their relationship, but she did acknowledge that, despite the growing business, they were not living a bigger life. She wanted more out of life and so did Bevan.

Bevan was the face of the business, the 'go to guy' when things went wrong or needed attention. Bevan was consumed by the business. He attended to all of the details. He had all of the technical knowledge to keep his business running.

The problem for him was that there was no escape from the business. The only escape would be to one day sell the business and take a long earned break.

I'm totally against that type of thinking. It's the 8th day of the week thinking: Work hard, slog your guts out for a few years then sell it, take a break and start the process all over again.

The problem with that is that bad habits get created along the way that never get broken until a crisis hits you.

What types of bad habits come from the 8th day of the week mentality?

The habit of not taking notice of your health, your spouse, your kids, your parents, your siblings, your friends, your hobbies and your investments. You end up becoming an expert at only taking notice of the business and trying to make more.

And yes, you do get more! More stress, more distance from loved ones, more complexities, more sleepless nights, more health issues, more confusion - more of everything except what you really want out of your life.

I believe that with LESS of the wrong habits you get MORE of the right habits.

Bevan and Julie understood this and it's why they came in to see me after so many years.

There's always a moment when you sit down with a client and you notice in their face and in their body language that there was something you said that really hit home for them.

Bevan was ready for the 24-Hour Human Battery strategy.

Hopefully you will be too.

I was standing next to Bevan when I went behind his back and said to him, 'Bevan. Imagine that right here, in the middle of your back, there is a human battery and it only lasts twenty-four hours.'
He said, 'Twenty-four hours a day?'

I said, 'NO, 24 hours in a WEEK! And once the twenty-four hours is up, you are magically stopped from doing any more business work until the following week, when you get another twenty-four hours of battery life to get through the next week.'

Bevan fired back at me, 'That's crazy. I'd never get everything done!'

And I calmly responded, in a hush-hush tone, 'Bingo! Do you think knowing that you only have twenty-four hours of battery time each week will force you to think and do things differently the following week?

Do you think you will re-consider what you say 'yes' to and 'no' to every week? Do you think that knowing your business battery will only last twenty-four hours this week will make you focus more, help you to get distracted less, force you to attend to all of the critical impact work that must get done every week, and keep you from mucking around with time-wasting stuff or people?'

His answer was a resounding, 'YES, YES, YES!'

The 24-Hour Human Battery exists in all business owners. It just hasn't been turned on in the right way.

When you do, you will almost magically get so much more done in a much shorter time. You will enjoy a load more Green Days™ (days of no business). Your health will improve, your cash flow will improve, your relationships will improve and ultimately your happiness levels will improve.

Unfortunately, most business owners think their battery lasts 168 hours a week (7 days x 24 hours per day), that their relationships will last forever, that their health will last forever, and because of that they are always thinking and doing business. But ultimately all it brings back to them is high stress and low profits.

As you already know, the formula for working smarter not harder is called 24-170®. The '24' part of it is to work a MAXIMUM of twenty-four hours a week. It's the 24-Hour Human Battery strategy in play.

What would you do differently if you knew you only had a maximum of 24 hours available to you in a week?

Your answer is your key to working less and achieving more.
Try it now:

'This is what I would do differently if I only had a maximum of 24 business hours available to me in a week.'

Lesson 8: Don't Do 10-Cent Activities

'Because we fear failure, we tend to do activities that we know we can do.'

To satisfy my curiosity I once asked a seven year old what was more valuable, 10-cents or $100,000? She answered, '$100,000 of course!'

You couldn't believe how happy I was with her answer.

Why?

Well, if a seven year old knows the difference between 10-cents and $100,000 then why on earth do adult business owners get distracted with 10-cent activities?

Before I answer with a WHY, let's look at WHAT 10-cent activities are.

A classic 10-cent activity is when you sit down to strategise how to get your customers to come back more often, and in the process you decide to quickly check that social media message that came in.

It's when you count the stock on the shelves instead of strategizing how to move it off the shelf quicker.

It's when you decide to wipe down your laptop or sort out your cupboard instead of investing that time on $100,000 activities.

I tell my clients that they are only one activity away from a $100,000 result, so why bother doing 10-cent activities?

So here's my take on WHY we prefer to get distracted with 10-cent ones:

At an early age we get rewarded for being busy. Teachers hate idle students, so we quickly learn to be occupied with work. Head down, tail up was the way to show your teacher that you were at least trying hard, and if you try hard you will get ahead. (I'm not sure what 'getting ahead' really meant as no one bothered to define that for us as kids, but that's another story).

In school we got rewarded for the right answers and were scolded for the wrong ones.

Right answers = Smiles, smugness, proudness and feelings of superiority.
Wrong answers = Anger, frustration, disbelief, jealousy and feelings of inferiority.

Because we fear failure, we tend to do activities that we know we can do. That's where 10-cent activities come into the picture.

We know how to do 10-cent activities. We don't really know how to do $100,000 activities.

The key strategy here is to do what you most fear.

Unlike when you were a pupil in school, as a business owner, you make up the rules and the punishment.

For me there is no punishment. If I make an error, the error is a learning message, it is a guiding error towards my next $100,000.

10-cent activities lead to 10-cent outcomes. $100,000 activities lead to $100,000 outcomes. It's your choice.

Once you know how to do $100,000 activities, you learn how to do $1 million activities. Once you know how to do $1 million activities, you learn how to do $10 million activities and so on.

From now on, every time you catch yourself doing a 10-cent activity ask yourself, 'What am I fearing that distracts me with 10-cent activities?'

That will be your answer to what needs to be done to get to your next $100,000 level in your business.

Lesson 9: Where's My Desk Gone?

'High quality relationships are not
built around a desk.'

In the 8th day of the week mentality the business owner loves their desk.

It's a monument to their level of importance - a status symbol even.

The bigger, more complex the desk, the more important and confident they feel. It gives them a place to feel secure and feel in control.

A desk is where a lot of '10-cent' activities occur, as business owners end up doing things which they know they can do, but are not really of any growth value to the business.

A desk is a great place to check emails, respond to emails, browse the web for hours looking for things, pile up physical mail, documents, brochures and folders.

It's also a great place to procrastinate, where 'knee-jerk reaction' things get done, while important things pile up.

A desk is bad for business. It's not for you. As a business owner you were never meant to have a desk. Desks are for tacticians who implement your strategies and even then, I would encourage them to use a stand-up desk instead.

A desk deteriorates your postural muscles. It's great for creating a sore neck, a curved back and slouching shoulders. It slows down activity, and it stifles creativity. Research has shown that your chance of an early death increases if you sit at a desk for very long periods.

So what do I use instead of a desk?

It depends.

If I am with a group of people working on a project, we go to a large enough table where we can lay out things and brainstorm. It doesn't have to be in an office. I prefer non-business settings, like a café, a home dining room or a picnic area. It shifts everyone's creativity and energy levels.

If I am working on a project alone, like I am right now writing this lesson, then I use a stand-up desk. I have my Red Day® Book with me (my personal and business project management system), a pen, my laptop and a 90 minute timer to make sure I don't work longer than 90 minutes in any given period.

With a stand-up desk, I am able to move around freely - I can think and move, stretch, twist and activate my core muscles to keep me upright and balanced. Have you noticed that when you are stuck on a problem, often just a short walk will help you get an answer?

We're meant to think while we are moving. It's very hard to move while sitting at a desk. It's very hard to come up with solutions to your business problems sitting at a desk.

You have to try it. It looks strange at first to outsiders, but I can honestly say that it has helped me dramatically reduce my back pain and get so much more quality work done.

I don't have any in-trays, no cabinets, no paper lying around - nothing but what I mentioned earlier. And here is the beauty of it all: when I'm done with my project, I close everything up and leave a totally clean and empty room. It's therapeutic to the mind to have that visual cleanliness. It's also a great confidence builder to know that you are not bound to a desk for your results.

One of the most valuable activities you can do as a business owner and sales professional is to build relationships with people. High quality relationships are not built around a desk.

Try this:
Identify the biggest 20% of the relationships you have in your business and go out there and talk to them. Get rid of your desk for 14 days and do just that. Connect up with your top clients/prospects/centres of influence and see what comes of it. I assure you, you'll get rid of your desk in an instant on the 15th day.

My accountant did just that, except he didn't wait until the 15th day. He did it on the first day he heard about this lesson.

It's what I truly admire about him. Many people over-analyse an idea, and they do that as a habit over many things in their business. As a consequence they delay progress. They become their own worst enemies in moving their business forward.

Here's what my accountant did:

Despite having a schedule full of client appointments the next day, it didn't stop him from removing his desk, removing all shelving, removing all cabinets and removing all traces of paperwork. All he had left in the room was his trusty whiteboard on the wall and four chairs. No desk.

He went into his first client meeting a bit apprehensive about how it would be perceived by his clients.

At first glance I am sure his clients might have thought that he was finding business tough and was selling everything. Once they got over the shock of their accountant not having a desk to talk over and he had explained the changes, they actually relaxed and opened up to him a lot more than they ever did previously.

The desk barrier was gone.

But more importantly, his clients now see their accountant as part of their team, brainstorming solutions together in an open environment - not an 'us vs. them' desk mentality.
Has this strategy worked for my accountant?

Well, let me share this much with you without embarrassing him.

He has restructured his business so that he doesn't have to work more than 15 hours a week in it. He has been featured in our prestigious business magazine called 'Business Review Weekly' twice for his successes in the accountancy industry and has become a self made multi-millionaire.

So where's your desk going?

Lesson 10: Why Do Customers Delay Their Decisions?

'We react in a fear and doubt mode
when we are unsure of our
environment.'

Marcus, a good friend of mine, is always on the look out for a better way: a better way of doing business, a better way of doing health, a better way of doing exercise. You name it, he loves finding a better way - it's what I admire most about him. He just loves to help people and he loves to refer business.

The problem I have with referrals in the 8th day mentality is that it happens way too slowly. With the 8th day mentality, we think it's okay to work crazy, long hours and, as a result, we also think it's okay for referrals to happen slowly.

As you already know, I only work twenty-four hours a week, so I need my referral business to come in faster. Much, much faster. And in order for you to make that happen you're going to need a lesson in human psychology.

That lesson comes in the form of sharing a recent event with you:

Marcus knows I love to play golf and, there was a time when I was having some back issues which was seriously affecting my game. So Marcus referred me to a guy called Adam.

Now, Adam is the go-to guy for the up and coming golfing elite. He is not a professional golfer, himself, he is a human movement expert and good golf is all about good body movement.

On no less than four occasions Marcus suggested that I go and see Adam. On one occasion he gave me Adam's business card and said I should ring him. On another occasion he sent me a Facebook message with a link to Adam's Facebook page.

You would have thought that, with my poor golf results and Marcus's recommendations over the past two months, I would have booked in to see Adam by this point.

I hadn't.

And that's got to beg the question: Why not?

Why, after receiving so many recommendations hadn't I booked in?

The answer came when Marcus and I were on the phone one day. He called me for an unrelated matter and, during the call, Marcus asked me if I had booked in to see Adam.

In that instant I knew I couldn't hide any longer. I had to fess up. I said to Marcus, 'No… but I want to share with you why I haven't made that call to see Adam.'

I could sense by the pause in our conversation that Marcus was really intrigued about what I was going to say next.

I told him that I was not sure if I would be able to commit myself and my time to following through with his exercise programme, that I feared letting him and Adam down as a result.

In short, I didn't want this to be another fad, where I get all excited about starting, but then get overwhelmed by what I've got to do and, in the process, give up.

To avoid any possible humiliation, it was easier for me to simply ignore Marcus's recommendations.

During this phone call with Marcus, I had an 'AHA' moment.

Could it be that my prospective 8th day of the week coaching clients could be thinking the same thing?

Could it be that *your* prospective clients could be thinking or fearing the same thing about doing business with you too?

Since all of our clients are human, the answer is most likely, 'YES!'

Marcus asked me an important question:

'What could Adam's business have done to reduce or ultimately eliminate your fears and doubts of booking in with him?'

In other words, Marcus was asking, 'How could Adam multiply the speed of growing his business and break out of the 8th day mentality of working harder, and not smarter, to grow his business?

It's a good question. In fact, it was an awesome question. Go back now and ask yourself the same question.

Here's my solution:

We react in a fear and doubt mode when we are unsure of our environment. This type of reaction is hardwired into us. It's a kneejerk reaction to the unknown. But when we became familiar with our surroundings, we start to reduce our fears and decrease our doubts.

The faster you can do this, the faster you will build your business and your referral business.

A referrer can only say so much about your business - they don't have all the answers. You've got to make it easy for the referrer to make that referral.

Here's what I would do as a start:

You need two things: a video and a webpage.

Direct ALL of your referrals to a webpage.

On that webpage you have a short video explaining what it is you do, how you do it and, MOST importantly, the fears and doubts most people have about taking their first step with you.

You will explain the common fears and how you help them through them. You will explain the common doubts and how you eradicate them.

In essence, you are making your referrals comfortable with their new environment, which speeds up your prospects' decision to do business with you.

When you don't buy into the 8th day of the week mentality and work as if you only have twenty-four hours for business work this week, it is amazing what solutions you can come up with in order to speed up your business results.

This is where more hours does not equal more results - FEWER hours equals more results, and that's how you break free of the 8th day of the week syndrome.

Lesson 11: Don't Be A Heavy Cloud

'Your business reflects YOU.'

Have you noticed that, when the sun is shining and the skies are blue all the way to the horizon, and when there's a warm, caressing breeze in the air, all of the sudden you gain a little skip in your step?

Okay, maybe not a skip, but you know what I mean. On days that look magical you feel different - your level of optimism, confidence and happiness seems to increase all of a sudden.

What you're experiencing on such a day is not actually magical - it's biological.

As humans, whether we are the business owner or business employees, the weather affects us. Sunshine, or simply light, can reduce people's level of depression, and, believe me, working an 8 day week with little or no natural sunlight is a recipe for a biological disaster.

In my early twenties I was developing a menswear boutique business.

I was the first to work and the last to leave.

I would even have my employees grab my lunch for me. I was the business owner remember, so I had a lot of responsibilities and a vast amount of things to take care of that only I could do - lunch was more of an interruption to my day than a break.

I rarely saw daylight and I developed a bad habit of thinking that this was normal. I also developed an intermittent sore throat.

I'd go to the late night doctor's clinic, as there was no time during the day - I was a busy man, I was the boss. The good old doc would look down my throat and raise his eyebrows hinting at the fact that things weren't looking too good down there.

'You have swollen tonsils.' He informed me with depressing regularity, 'I can give you antibiotics, but if it continues like this, you'd be better off having them taken out.'

Remove my tonsils? I thought, 'That's not a bad idea. It would stop all these late night visits to the docs, the fevers, and the aches and pains I'd get throughout the day.'

But then I realized that this would mean going to hospital and being bedridden for a few days. I couldn't afford that sort of time off! This is, of course, the way 8th day of the week business owners think.

And so I'd tell him, 'Forget it, doc. Give me the antibiotics!'

As a consequence of trying to achieve more, we convince ourselves that we don't have time to do the right thing, opting instead for a quick fix. The most common option for an 8th day of the week business owner is the path of least interruption to the day.

The 8th day of the week work ethic doesn't make us better, it makes us worse on so many levels!

Don't get me wrong. It's not that an 8th day of the weeker can't make a lot of money, they can. But you have to ask yourself at 'what cost?'.

Side Note:
It always amuses me how people work hard all of their lives, missing out on good health, good relationships, good time away only to retire and then spend all of their hard earned money trying

to stay alive and away from hospitals and doctors. It's the ultimate human irony. And it should never be that way, not for business owners or employees. We've been sold a big lie. Don't buy into it.

Back to my sore throat.

I kept taking the antibiotics and that kept me at a level of being JUST able to continue my 8th Day working mentality.

Over time, my body became tired and I became tired. I needed a solution and fast.

Being an 8th day of the week thinker, everything had to be done fast and with the least interruption to my business schedule.

A day off away from work simply meant I had double the amount to do the next day.

On one occasion I booked into see my doctor again - wanting to do so for a couple of reasons. One was to complain again about my sore throat and the other was to question the type of antibiotics I was on. As fate would have it, my usual doctor was unavailable the night I booked in.

My replacement doctor was a lot older than my usual one. He looked more like Father Christmas to me - he had a big bushy beard, small spectacles and a biggish nose. But he was softly spoken and very direct.

He asked me where I worked and at what time I started and finished my day. He also wanted to know if I had lunch inside or outside of my menswear store.

Before I answered, I fired back, 'What's that got to do with my tonsillitis?'

He fired back in turn, 'I'm the doctor, I ask the questions. You're the patient, you answer the questions - that's how it works here.'

I quickly replied. 'I get up early - always the first to work and the last to leave, usually eight in the morning to nine at night, and since I skip lunch most days, I drive through the closest fast food outlet and eat while I'm driving home.'

'Okay,' said the doc, 'Here's what I want you to do. Stop all the antibiotics. take a minimum of thirty minutes for lunch and make sure you have your lunch outside, in the open air. I want you to have at least half an hour of sunlight every day. That will fix your sore throat. If you don't do this, I will see you back here for an appointment to meet with an ear, nose, and throat surgeon, who will remove your tonsils. Just keep in mind that there is no guarantee that, even after the operation, you won't still be getting a sore throat. Understood?'

'Yep.' I said.

'Good, now go home and make sure you enjoy the sunlight everyday.' He said with a faint smile.

I admire people who can give advice like that. To the point, full of confidence and contrary to what everyone else was saying to me. And it felt good hearing it.

Deep down, I was craving for what he had prescribed me. - more sunlight and no medicines!

It was music to my ears and my body. But sometimes you just need to be at that point of listening.

The 8th day of the week mentality blocks out ALL good advice. You just get too busy to be healthy and eventually the neglect catches up with you. It always does.

Right now I am living in a place, aptly named, the Sunshine Coast. It's the middle of August - the middle of our winter - and it's going to be twenty-six degrees Celsius (78.8 degrees Fahrenheit) today. Now that is purely magical. I love it!

Last week, I had a 'Coffee Session' (I don't call them consultations) with Jake, a dear friend and client of mine. He is developing an electrical contracting business. As we were about to sit down, I mentioned to Jake that he must be loving the great winter weather we've been having lately.

He replied with something that reminded me of that conversation with the doc over twenty years ago.

'George,' he said, 'it's been fantastic, you know. There's a buzz in the air, the boys (his employees) are just so much more happier when the weather's like this.'

And he was spot on. Good weather DOES make you feel better, and when you feel better, you work better, your businesses results are better - it's as simple as that.

Where I live, our winters are dry and cool, while our summers are wet and humid.

It's typical subtropical living. But of late our weather hasn't been very typical. We've been experiencing a very wet winter. This can have the effect of throwing us completely out of sync.

It's been five days since I had that Coffee Session with Jake and his wife, Jenny. I thought about his comment on how the good weather had changed the energy of his team, how they were working faster, more happily.

There was a positive and also a clear negative to what he said.

Yes, it's great that the good weather produced better energy within the team, which means they get more work done as a result - working through any problems they face a lot quicker, so the jobs become more profitable.

BUT, what will happen to all of this when the weather turns bad again?

Well, we know that we can't control the 'external sunshine', and this got me thinking - is there such a thing as 'internal sunshine'? And if there is, can we control it?

I have to answer these questions with a resounding 'YES!' and 'YES!'

External sunshine gives the planet energy to live and to thrive. But what happens to our workplace when there is no sunshine to speak of for a day, a week, a month, a quarter or even a whole year? Then what?

That's when we need to create our own 'internal sunshine', regardless of what the weather is doing to us externally.

How does this work in your business?

Your business reflects YOU.

Consider this: if you walk in all grumpy and down, no matter how positive your employees are, you will dampen their mood in an instant. You become the big, dark cloud!

It's the same effect that we feel when the sun disappears behind a cloud. We go from warm and excited to cold and worried.

You are the internal sunshine or the internal cloud -it's your choice.

If you're thinking that a sour face communicates to your employees that they had better not be slacking off when you're not around, then you've not worked out how we humans work best.

I'm not saying you should be the internal sunshine even when an employee has broken the company rules - be a cloud then - but don't be a cloud all of the time. Eventually everyone in the business will leave, even your partner, because no one can stand bad weather indefinitely - not when there are other, more sunny options available.

Working in an 8th day framework ensures that you almost always bring internal clouds to your workplace.

Think about it.

You're tired, no one has worked as hard or as long as you. The bills are mounting, the cash flow is always stretched, the customers are demanding and the employees can't live up to your expectations. Of course you're going to go to work the next day as the internal cloud.

Break free from the 8th day mentality and watch how you transform to become the internal sunshine at your business and how that not only keeps your best employees, but also attracts other talent who are running away from their boss's black cloud thinking.

This is what Jake has decided to do as a result of this strategy:

It's important for Jake that his team starts off the day in good spirits.

So, when the weather outside is bad, Jake now comes into the workplace with their favourite muffins bought from the local store.

You should see the energy change in everyone's face when they see Jake walk in. They have a twelve minute, stand up meeting to go over the day's schedule with him and his wife, Jenny, they all get to eat their muffins, have a warm drink and then head off for the day.

Jake was the internal sunshine they were missing. Jake has full control of his business' internal weather. So do you.

People around you will do more for you and your business without introducing penalties and harsh consequences when you turn on the internal sunshine for them.

Make it a new habit and watch how your business achieves more with less effort by you. It's another way of breaking free from the 8th day of the week.

Lesson 12: Coping With Good Run Anxiety

'You can only control the controllables,
let go of everything else.'

Have you ever had the feeling that everything is going well... too well, in fact - and you're waiting for something bad to happen, something that you haven't accounted for, something that will break this good run?

How should you go about handling that type of feeling?

Should you worry about whatever it is that might happen, what might be coming up or what might be around the corner?

Or

Should you embrace the good run and be wise enough to know that all good runs, and therefore all bad runs, never last forever?

I have consulted with so many business owners that I can tell you categorically that not only *should* you embrace the good runs to the fullest, but you MUST embrace them to the fullest. And here's why:

When a bad run hits - and it always does - see it for what it is, then deal with it, get through it, learn from it, discover the opportunities it presents, and then get ready to enjoy your next good run. After all, they always come about too.

If you're into golf, you're going to love this analogy. If you've tried golf and don't like it, this might well change your mind - at the very least you'll learn an extremely powerful success technique, which I've used and shared with my small business owners.

I want you to imagine that you're at one of the most beautiful golf courses on the planet.

I want you to imagine that you're stepping up to a par three hole (par = the number of shots a first-class player should normally require for a particular hole).

It has a majestic view.

You've just walked onto the tee off box and you notice that it sits perched high above the green like an eagle hovering over its prey. It gives you a powerful, lofty feeling. It's 161 metres to the pin and simply breathtaking - the view, the height, the warm caressing breeze. It intoxicates you. BUT...

Between you and the green is an area known as 'Death Valley'. There's nothing there but molasses-thick, snake-ridden grassland, so thick that if your ball lands within an inch of its grasp, it is as good as consumed forever!

Up until this point you've had a good run - you've played some of your best ever golf - but now this beautiful, yet mentally menacing, par three is weaving fear and doubt into your psyche. You face it with the belief that this could be the hole that puts an end to your good run.

Now what?

You really have only two choices. Well, three really.

The first one is to stop playing. Walk away right now, knowing you've played one of your best rounds ever and don't risk what might happen next.

Some people do this in business. They are so scared that a good run in business will end in disaster that they just stop playing the game of business. They retreat and play instead a lesser game of 'safety'.

The second option is to step up and play your shot full of all of the hazards in your mind. You approach the markers on the tee off area and you clearly see the potential disaster that will end your good run. Now, your all consuming thought becomes, 'I've gotta hit this over Death Valley. I've gotta hit this over Death Valley...'

What do you think will happen?

Right! You'll most likely hit your ball straight into the hungry mouth of Death Valley. It knew you would and you knew you would - it was a foregone conclusion long before you even hit the damn ball!

People say 'positive thinking' will get you through such circumstances. I don't agree.

You can give yourself all the positive thoughts in the world before you hit the ball, but if the last thought that goes through your mind is, 'Don't go into Death Valley', that is exactly where your ball will end up.

Your third option, and it's the solution to coping with Good Run Anxiety and producing the best run you've ever had in business and in life, is the following:
Step up to the tee off area. Marvel at the expansive beauty of the hole including the beauty of the hazards, accepting that they are all part of the picture you are seeing.

Accept that it IS a possibility, that you MAY stuff up...and then LET GO.

Once you let go of the possibility (and it's a real possibility that you might stuff up), you are free to focus on the other possibility -

the possibility that you will hit one of the sweetest shots of your life, which is actually quite probable as you've been playing well so far anyway!

Accept that you're on a good run right now. No one knows how long it will last. And accept that bad runs are possible. Once you accept this as a possibility, you set yourself free to enjoy and embrace the good run that IS happening to you right now.

Accept the possibility, let go of it, free up your mind and let the good run continue.

To think anything else would defeat the reason you went into business: to have a bigger life.

You can only control the controllables, let go of everything else.

There can be no bigger life if your time is spent worrying about something that is out of your control.

Lesson 13: What's Possible Is Not Always Probable

'It takes approximately ten years or ten thousand hours to become an expert in any field.'

Could I learn to speak fluent Hindi in seven days?

My answer is a BIG NO!

Yes, I know, people always say to me: 'It IS possible George. Don't be so negative.' Well, on a scientific level I agree that it IS possible, BUT…

It's NOT highly probable!

You have to know the difference between what's possible and what's probable, if you want to seriously get out of the 8th day of the week mentality.

The 8th day weekers believe that anything is possible. And it is. But, in the same way, not everything is highly probable.

Wishful thinking is just that - wishful.

Positive thinking is just that - positive.

Wishful and positive thinking are like two well-meaning friends, but they don't pay the bills for you.

Is it possible that I could double my sales overnight?

Yes, of course it's possible. But it's not probable… UNLESS I do three things:

---

1. I change what I know, and practice it.
2. I change the people I surround myself with, and practice with them
3. I change the activities I give my time to, and practice them.

You'll notice two key words are repeated here: 'change' and 'practice'.

If you are serious about making something more probable, you'll have to change what you are doing and practice it over and over and over again.

Professor Anders Ericsson is the expert on experts. In his ground-breaking study, he discovered that it takes approximately ten years or ten thousand hours to become an expert in any field.

But, here's the real key behind what he says:

Let's say you want to become a really, really good golfer. Maybe even a pro tour player.

According to this research, having played golf for ten years won't qualify you as an expert. Far from it! You may have been practicing *incorrectly* for those ten years and become worse.

To become an expert, you would have had to have put in at least ten thousand hours of 'Deliberate Practice'. That's a minimum of twenty hours per week for ten years, or you could do it in five years if you put in forty hours a week.

So what is 'Deliberate Practice'?

Well, lets go back to the golfing example.

Hitting a bucket of balls at the driving range for an hour is simply practice. It's not Deliberate Practice, it's just practice, which is okay if you want to remain average.

On the other hand, if you hit a bucket of balls with your nine iron at a specific target until 80% of the balls land within two metres of that target, this is what Professor Ericsson is talking about.

This is what Deliberate Practice is all about and it does require you to be open to accepting outside help - a coach, someone who can get you practicing deliberately.

Musicians do it, tennis players do it, cricketers do it, footballers do it, politicians do it, millionaires and billionaires do it, artists do it, writers do it - all the greats, he has found, have done the minimum ten years or ten thousand hours of Deliberate Practice.

That's how you turn possible into probable!

Clever marketing would have us believe that everything is possible TODAY, not just in ten years' time.

'NOW' and 'INSTANT' have become the ruthless marketer's weapons used to appeal to the desperate and the needy. They promise to sell you stuff that bypasses any need for 'Deliberate Practice'.

A doctor's office is called a 'practice', because that's where they practice their art of medicine. Eventually, with enough Deliberate Practice, they could qualify to become a 'specialist' or an expert in a specific field.

You won't find a doctor who is an expert in ALL fields of medicine. Why? Because they don't have enough 'ten thousand hours' in their life to qualify.

Nor do you.

Who gets paid more: a general doctor or a specialist? You get the picture.

You can't become an expert in all areas of running your business. Instead, you have to become an expert in ONE aspect of your business and hire other talented people to do the rest with and for you.

8th day of the weekers believe they have to do everything, and, as a result, they only produce weak, stressful outcomes.

For your business to truly grow and prosper you need to <u>develop</u> the business. So your main role, as an owner of a business, is to be the business developer.

In the 24-170® business developers model, Red Days® are our special days - the ones we put aside for developing our business.

A Red Day® is a day, or a number of hours in a day, which we put aside as uninterrupted time to work ON the business.

We look for ways to add more control, more growth and more leverage to what we do so that we can create raving fans out of our customers and our team members.

Here's the great part of doing all of this:
You don't need ten years or ten thousand hours of Deliberate Practice to become a highly profitable business developer.

Unlike a golfer, who may or may not make any money for the first five to seven years of their career, you, as a business developer, can be making very decent profits in your first year of business.

That, I know, is highly <u>probable</u>.

Making millions in your first year or even hundreds of thousands in your first year is possible, but it's not probable.

If you find that hard news to swallow, go back to the above three points I mentioned earlier and review this lesson again. It's the key to moving forward happily.

Lesson 14: Ambition Vs. Ability – Don't Confuse Them

'They need to be surrounded by implementers!
They need people UNLIKE themselves.'

What is your AMBITION?

What ABILITY do you possess that will ensure you achieve your ambition?

8th day of the weekers typically paint big, ambitious pictures for themselves and their families.

In that picture they see themselves having more. More of everything.

More possessions, more wealth, more relationships, more free time, more control and more experiences. More of a bigger and better life.

Ironically, it doesn't end up like that… but they do get MORE.

More health issues, more body weight, more financial complexities, more debt, more people problems, more time spent in the business, more time away from family, more worries and more daily stresses.

Why?

8th day of the weekers tend to be far right brainers - they have great ideas, but they struggle big time at consistently implementing their ideas.

Solution:
They need to be surrounded by implementers!

They need people UNLIKE themselves.

Some business owners never get this lesson and continue to run and control the business as though they are the only ones who can do what needs to be done.

Let's go back for a business lesson on the golf course.

I'm a right brainer and I love golf. So here is my strategy, which I used in the early days to help me play well:

Before a competition, I would lay in bed the night before and visualize how I was going to play every single hole.

I would go through each hole, visualizing what club I was going to pull out of the bag, picturing the distance the ball would travel and where it would land, considering my next shot and imagining exactly what would happen once I reached the putting green.

In my mind I played near-perfect golf. I was a champ! That was my AMBITION.

I'd spring out of bed the next day, all excited and pumped up. I'd look out of the window and, if it was a clear sunny day, I would convince myself that today was going to be MY day of victory - the golfing gods were going to be on my side.

I totally felt that, today, I was going to play my best round ever. It would be so good, in fact, that the TV stations, newspapers and golfing journals would be scrambling to interview me, asking me how I did it, what I ate in the morning and what my secret was. I could even see what the papers headline would read:

'Amateur Golfer Discovers The Secret To Pro Golf Scores'

In my mind I was expressing my AMBITION to myself.

I turn up to the golf course, pumped up, with all the thoughts of how I was going to play today still racing through my mind - still quietly confident that today was my day.

I step up to the first tee, a bit nervous, but silently excited, and with one glorious swing I smash the ball right out of bounds! With a one stroke penalty, and now hitting my second ball, I haven't even moved off the tee box and my score is already three for a par four. In the end, I finish with a seven.

My mind then goes into a tail spin. This is not what was meant to happen! At this point there is a huge conflict going on in between my ears.

It's at just such moments that I realise my AMBITION does not match my REALITY. There is a huge gap between the two!

I carry on, telling myself there's plenty of holes left, and that it was just probably nerves. I continue playing, hoping that the next hole will match my ambition.

It doesn't!

I ended up with one of my worst rounds for the year.

It's crushing for my ego and my sanity. I question my ambitions, but quickly shrug it off by telling myself that it was just 'one of those rounds' and there's always next week.

Business owners play the game of business in much the same way that they play the game of golf.

They have huge ambitions, but their abilities don't match those ambitions.

This is a very serious problem.

The problem is that when your ambitions (or goals) don't match your abilities (business skills), the kneejerk reaction is to compensate by working harder and harder and harder until you simply can't do it anymore.

We play more golf, we go to the driving range and hit hundreds of balls, but nothing really changes except that we get tired and disillusioned with the game of golf and, more importantly, with ourselves.

With this type of thinking, business owners end up either selling their business (selling their golf clubs) or closing the business down (giving away their golf clubs).

If I was serious about my golfing ambitions, as you should be about your business ambitions, then all I needed to do is find people to help me bridge the gap between my ambitions and my abilities.

To became a better golfer I needed to up my golfing skills. I took a series of lessons, had my golf clubs custom fitted and practiced over and over again. I studied what it took not only to play better golf, but also to think better around the course, so that I could play with strategic purpose instead of just trying to whack the ball as close as possible to the hole.

I tamed down my ambitions to match my current abilities. If I played within one or two strokes of my handicap, I would tell myself it was a great round. I would also tell myself that, if I wanted to play below my handicap, I would have to get more coaching and practice in so that I could bridge the real gap between my ambition and my ability.

Business is no different.

Be real about your current abilities and be real about your ambitions. If there is a gap, bridge it.

Working longer and harder hours won't bridge the gap.

If you confuse your ambitions with your abilities you will need a very strong pair of legs, because you'll be doing a lot of running around and time wasting, and that's how you end up working the 8th day of the week.

Seek support, mentors and coaches who can help you bridge the gap between your ambitions and your current abilities.

Lesson 15: Trust – Let Go – Enjoy

'It wasn't 'hard work' - it was 'solid, focused work' - there is a big difference between the two!'

Last year, when I entered my golf club's annual championships, I tried to win purely on the basis of my 'rugged individualism'.

The result: I had my worst four rounds of the year, failing to break a hundred once in the four day competition. But not this year...

The following *true* golfing story has helped many business owners apply my mantra of 'Trust-Let Go-Enjoy' to smash their way out of the 8th day of the week trap. My wish is that it will do the same for you.

This lesson is perfect for business owners who have trouble trusting, letting go and enjoying.

In the five weeks prior to the club championships I decided to apply the Red Day® business coaching strategies to my golf game. I pulled out one of the tools I give to my clients: 'The Ultimate Goal Achievement Strategy'.

You might assume that I would have written, 'Win the club championships' as the title of my passionate goal. I didn't. In fact, the words 'club championship' weren't even mentioned.

My passionate goal was to shoot one game at eight under my current handicap (the lower your golfing handicap, the better the player you are.) within 90 days, and I had four specific milestones that I needed to reach in order to do that.

There were also three inevitable achievement actions I had to take in order achieve my passionate goal.

I upgraded my equipment, got coached twice a week, detached myself from expectations, bridged the gap between my ambitions and abilities, and I relied on trusting, letting go and enjoying the whole process.

It wasn't 'hard work' - it was 'solid, focused work' - there is a big difference between the two!

Working HARD to me implies slogging it out, working SOLID implies concentrated, uninterrupted, focused and effective work.

Golf requires a solid swing, all the greats of golf will tell you that. They'll also tell you that a hard swing is a recipe for disaster.

Solid work trumps hard work anytime!

My Results:

I shot exactly forty-three FEWER strokes than I did last year - an average of eleven strokes per round DECREASE. I played my best two rounds of the year so far (and under championship conditions, in very gusty winds). My handicap almost dropped by two strokes during the four day tournament.

At home I had 100% support from my spouse to go out, practice and play without any guilt about being obsessed and being away too often. In fact, I made her an important part of achieving my goal - she happily agreed to keep me accountable to what I had promised to do.

Here's how I turned things around:

I was leading after day one, day two and day three of the four day tournament. My mate told me I had an eight-stroke lead going into the final fourth day.

I didn't feel like I had the magic when I woke up for the final day's play. I headed off to the driving range for a half hour warm up, but I didn't feel right. I wasn't hitting my clubs crisply like I had done the day before.

The pressure of winning and possibly losing was creeping into my psyche.

All of the Red Day® lessons were now most on my mind. If I was to win, I had to let go and detach myself, which is always easier said than done.

I met my three fellow competitors that made up the group for the final day's pairings. I had neither met nor played with any of them before.

I hit a lousy shot off the first tee (a par four) - straight into the trees on the left. All of the others landed theirs in safe open areas.

I was kicking myself for not living up to my expectations after the first tee shot. I mean, I was supposed to show these guys why I was the leader, right?

'EXPECTATIONS are your enemy, George.' I told myself, as I walked off to find my ball, 'DETACHMENT is your ally.'
I had a lousy lie for my second shot, hindered by trees and thick scrub. I opted to go for safety and punched the ball out with my five iron.

Now, I had a chance to get the ball on the green for three. The pin was placed neatly behind a huge sand bunker - it's what we call a 'sucker pin' placement, it's put there to lure you to go for the hole. The penalty for getting it wrong is that you either end up in the bunker or you overshoot the pin, ending up down in a valley past the pin which makes for a very difficult chip back up.

This is where you have to play to your strengths. The club I had been most accurate with, during my warm up at the driving range, was my eight iron and it was exactly an eight iron shot to the flag. I went for it, full of confidence, and nailed my third shot, leaving the ball eight feet from the hole. I read the green from both sides and nailed the putt for a par.

The next hole was a par five. With three solid shots and two putts, I nailed that one too. I can't say I was feeling confident though - I was still doubting myself even after paring the first two holes.

The next six holes were my worst of the tournament. I double and triple bogeyed. My brain went from a tail spin of denial ('This can't be happening!') to an, 'Okay, accept that this may be your worst round ever and let go.'

There was a real conflict going on. I kept repeating this statement in my mind, but then thought that, if I had to keep repeating it, I didn't believe it - it had to be said once and then let go. Only then would I have believed in what I was telling myself.

I fought with this conflict for a further three holes and things failed to improve. Finally, I had had enough and really let go. I was finally at 'PNR – the Point of No Return'. I let go of all the negative consequences, the fears and the doubts…I conceded mentally that I could lose the whole championship.

I added up my partner's score and mine for the first nine. We do this for a couple of reasons - firstly to make sure there are no errors in our scoring so far (handing in an incorrectly scored card can mean you get instantly disqualified!), and secondly to track how we are doing and gauge our score against each other.
As I added up my score, I knew it wasn't going to be good… and it wasn't. It was the worst score of the four of us. This made me

angry yet super focused.

We all walked over to the tenth tee. This was the home stretch - nine holes to play and it would all be over.

I reminded myself that my last nine holes had no connection with how I was going to play the next nine holes, unless I wanted to connect them in any way. I chose to view them as two completely separate rounds.

I blocked out my competitors - it was as if I was playing alone and all I can remember now is that I focused on making my next shot, my next shot and my next shot...

Finally, we were all standing together on the eighteenth hole, our clubs 'signature' hole. It is a 146 metre, par three. There is a huge valley (members call it the 'Valley of Death') between the tee off area and the green - you have to fly the ball on the full all the way from the tee off box to the green. Anything short of this and you're in trouble.

Being the finishing hole, I was worried about it from the start of the day's play, but by the end of the round I told myself I was going to nail the hole!

I approached the tee, having made sure I was going to shoot first out of our group - I wanted to show them what they had to chase.

I took out my six iron and got into a hyper-focused zone. This helped me block out the crowd of spectators at the eighteenth hole, who were heckling the players (all in good fun). I shot the ball straight at the pin, and it almost hit it.

It skirted past the pin onto the cuff of the green, but it meant I finished the hole with a par and with cheers from the gallery. In the end, I won by three strokes, becoming the clubs C-Grade

Champion of the year.

LESSON: when you are leading after day one, day two, day three, it is very hard to let go of expectations on day four. But not letting go of expectations, whether implicit or explicit, will stop the flow and hinder you winning on day four.

The bigger and more successful you become in business the harder it can be to let go of expecting yourself to continue to be more successful. Not letting go of those expectations can stop your flow and trigger your downfall.

It is much more difficult to let go when you are already at the top - it's why the underdogs usually come in from nowhere and win. They are detached from the result. They free themselves up to become hyper focused on their strengths instead of on their expectations.

You don't learn to let go when you're at the top of your game - you let go from the beginning so that you can get to the top of your game.

You can't let go unless you learn to trust and, when you trust, you can't help but enjoy the journey not only of your business, but also of your life.

Trust – Let Go – Enjoy.

Lesson 16: What You Eat And Drink Can Destroy Your Business

"Knowing' something doesn't mean
we change our behaviour.'

You might be thinking that I've gone a bit far here with the headline, but what if I told you that what you eat and drink is a major cause for you working eight days of the week?

That it is causing you to have less growth in your business, less control over your business, and less time away from your business? Would you be prepared to listen if I offered to show you a better way?

I'm no nutritional scientist, but I did complete a minor in physiology and I do have a passion for the mind-body connection.

I'm also no super health freak. I have a weakness for chocolate coated anything and, because I know my weaknesses, I also know what I need to do to maintain a high level of focus and energy when it's most needed in my working week.

You know by now that I don't work more than twenty-four hours in a week and, if I slack off during my work day, my punishment is that I have to cancel my Green Day™ to complete my work. That is a very strong incentive for me to find better ways of staying hyper-focused, and to block out interruptions and the lure of doing 10-cent activities.

Over the years, I've observed business owners energy and focus levels.

I noticed that when we eat the wrong foods, our energy levels rise for a short while, but before long we crash and burn.

In myself I have noticed that my productivity and focus after a 'bad food' meal is all high and excited - my confidence rises, I become bulletproof, my ideas seem doable and my projections for the future become higher and brighter. Nothing seems to bother me...

But then comes the crash and burn.

What I just ate and drank was only good for about twenty minutes and after that I literally have to battle with a foggy brain, sluggishness, conflicting thoughts, lowered confidence, procrastination, irritation and even downright lowered self-esteem - all because of what I put in my gob!

It's like I am two different people jumping from one personality to the other, day in day out - all because of what I consumed.

The 8th day of the weeker, knows this cycle very well.

They also know what needs to be done. The problem is that they don't do it.

Because the last crash and burn they went through was so bad, and lasted for so long, they have been conditioned to crave the next dose of the bad food pick-me-up - they need the twenty minute rush. This makes the 'bad meal' highly addictive.

And that's how a vicious cycle starts.

24-170® is not only a 'work smarter not harder' formula, it is also a 'live happier not sadder' formula.

When you take your business towards the goal of 24-170®, your friends, spouse, kids and other family members will enjoy you - the REAL YOU - even more.

You are not you when you consume an 8th day of the weeker meal plan. You know it, your friends know it, your kids know it… but 'knowing' something doesn't mean we change our behaviour.

Continue this way of eating for the next meal, the next day, the next week, the next month, the next quarter, the next year, the next decade, and before you know it you and your business will burn out!

If you ever feel like you are two different types of people in your business day, you can bet it's all based on **what** you eat and drink, **when** you eat and drink and **how** you eat and drink.

You are a reflection of your business. If you are sluggish, I bet your response times to your customers are also sluggish. Your business is a mirror of you and your energy.

If you have employees, this sluggishness and burn out further multiplies if they too are eating poorly. Worse still, you're actually paying your employees to produce these sluggish results in your business. This results in you having to work longer hours.

I don't like to complicate things, even how to eat and drink, so here are my simplistic, yet highly effective, strategies to help you to get super-focused, energised and stay out of the 8th day of the week work syndrome:

WHAT & WHEN to eat and drink?

Firstly, don't confuse hunger for thirst.

We've become expertly conditioned to search for food when feeling hungry, but in fact the real need is always thirst. What your body really craves for is water.
So, next time you're feeling the desire for food, down two glasses of water and I bet your need for food will be reduced dramatically. So will your waistline!

Now, let's assume it's time to eat.

When you're facing a restaurant menu or the home fridge, ask yourself this one question, because it will tell you exactly what is wrong and what is right for you to be eating and drinking at that time of the day:

'Will this food and drink I am about to consume <u>increase</u> or <u>decrease</u> my energy and focus for the rest of the day?'

Even more powerful is to place your hand on your belly while you are asking that question - go on, re-read the question with your hand on your belly and notice the difference.

You'll probably end up laughing while you read it out, but that laughter is your mind's way of saying, 'it's true isn't it?'

By doing this you are not only asking your mind, but also your body, what would be the right choice. Your body knows. Your mind just needs to be reminded.

When should you ask yourself this potent question?

<u>Every time</u> you have the desire to eat, whether it be breakfast, lunch, dinner or any other time in between.

It's the most effective question to help lose weight and gain energy!

I am not going to go into what the right and wrong foods and drinks are here - it's different for everyone - but I will give you an example of how I do it in real life:
It's 9am. and I've already completed two 90-minute chunks of highly focused work. All I've had so far is a cup of tea and continuous sips of filtered water. I am naturally more alert and

focused early in the morning, so I take advantage of my body clock by rising early and getting straight into my day.

By 9am, I have done my best work. When I work like this I feel like I am in a time warp. 180 minutes feels like 15. I get into a hyper-focused state. It's, fun, exciting and valuable. It's also how I wrote this book.

But, by 9am my stomach and mind start to grumble for food.

There is a temptation to munch into the chocolate coated, custard filled profiteroles in the fridge, but I know I have another two ninety minute chunks of work time left and I want to stay energised and focused for that.

So for me, it's a mixed veggie omelette, a cup of tea and some grainy bread. I know from experience that this simple food and drink plan will keep me focused and energised for the next two ninety minute chunks.

The benefit of the quality of the work I will produce by staying energised and focused greatly outweighs my desire for the profiteroles. I crave my Green Days™ far more than my profiteroles, so for me it's a no brainer. If I struggle with the desire to munch into the profiteroles, I look at them, place my hand on my belly and ask myself that energy and focus question all over again.

Don't misunderstand me, I won't deprive myself of the profiteroles - they were bought for a reason. When I no longer need to be energised and hyper-focused, I'll sit down and consume one (or maybe even two!) slowly, enjoying every bite as a small reward for a great day. You should always reward yourself in some way and this is one way that I do it.

HOW to eat and drink?

What and when you eat and drink is crucial for your energy and focus levels, but in the western world we have forgotten about the importance of the HOW.

My wife was born in Jakarta, Indonesia. She is an entrepreneur in her own right. When I first met her she was also the queen of the 8th day of the week mantra. But, despite her hectic and long daily schedule, she always had a great way of having lunch with her employees.

She told me, 'We don't eat like you guys do in the western world.' She had noticed that, when westerners eat, they eat fast, often doing so while sitting with their computers, talking on their phones and even when watching TV.

'We never do that.' she said. 'You see, food for us is very precious and highly valued, so we always take time out just to eat.'

'We all sit close together with no phones, computers or anything like that in the room. We all laugh about the day or reflect on things that have happened or are about to happen in our lives – it connects us. We take time to chew our food, share our food and enjoy our food.

It's also a great opportunity to find out things that I need to be aware of. For example, I may hear that a teacher is planning a holiday or that someone is struggling in their personal life. This way I get a chance to understand them and help them.'

Her story made me reflect that, here in the western world; we have lost the art of **HOW to eat**. It's become more about rushing than it has about being nourished. And most of us have stopped eating in visually nourishing environments.

It's one reason I love working from home. When it's lunchtime, we prepare our lunch together as often as possible. There's something energetic about making your own meal - the preparation of it and the eating of it.

How you eat affects your short term and long term results in life.

The HOW impacts the speed at which you eat your food, the quality of your chewing. The Chinese have a wise saying: 'Your stomach has no teeth, chew slowly before you swallow.'

All of this affects how long your body's energy reserves will take to process your meal. The longer it takes, the longer it will take you to get re-focused and energised so you can complete your work.

We sit to eat our food, taking time to notice the tastes, the ingredients, the colours and the textures. We chitchat. We sit outside on nice days. We don't have the TV on, but eat away from all the trappings of technology and our phones are always on silent.

When you eat peacefully you notice things you never noticed before. The sounds of the birds, the colours of the leaves, the flowers, the wind speed, even the taste of your food!

This 'tuning in' is natural to us humans, but it gets washed out with the noise of electronics and emotional stress.

As an entrepreneur you have to stay tuned in - you have to be more 'present', so that you can see the opportunities in front of your nose together with the dangers as well.

If you eat too fast or in stressful environments, you'll find your energy and focus levels will slump.

I am a strong believer in Deepak Chopra's idea that you can eat a crappy diet in a happy home and it won't affect you as much as a person who eats the healthiest organic foods in a home of high stress. How you eat is as important, if not more important, than what you eat.

Get back into a natural state of what, when and how to eat and drink, and you will see how opportunities come about, not once in a lifetime, but anytime you want them to appear.

Lesson 17: Some Days I Just Lack Motivation And Feel 'Yuck'

*'When your body is not feeling well,
don't argue with it'*

There's something going on…

In the past five days alone, I've had three people tell me that they simply lack the motivation to get anything done. And, on top of that, they feel 'yuck!'

They also told me that, at the end of each day, they feel guilty for not having accomplished much. And this only makes things worse when they think about everything that needs to be done tomorrow.

That's just another way that the 8th day of the week syndrome begins.

This is what an 8th day of the weeker typically starts to think: 'Okay. I didn't do much today, so I've got to work my butt off tomorrow and if I don't these feelings of guilt will double. This means I'll have to work even harder the next day.'

Dangerous cycle? You bet!

Let's have a reality check:

Marketers and pharmaceutical companies will have us believe that, if we are not feeling on top of the world every day, then there is something wrong with us.

I don't buy into it.

When your body is not feeling well, don't argue with it - it's trying its best to tell you something. It's telling you to take it easy.

When your mind is not feeling in top form, don't argue with it - it's trying to tell you exactly the same thing: 'Take it easy.'

I had one business owner contact me and tell me that he was feeling overwhelmed and he simply didn't know what to do anymore.

He was making seriously good money and wasn't working long hours, but he had noticed that his passion for the business was dwindling like a late night campfire.

This worried him immensely. He was worried that it might be the start of his demise.

I discovered that he loved to exercise, so I focused on his deep understanding of the human body to help him understand his lack of motivation.

I asked him what he would do if his body was feeling tired and almost burnt out?

He replied immediately, without any hesitation, 'I'd simply take a few days off from exercising.'

Then I asked him, 'If your mind was feeling tired and almost burnt out, what would you do about it?'

He said, 'Well, I can't just take a few days off from thinking, can I?'

'Of course you can!' I replied.

You can't take a break from thinking altogether, but you can from certain types of thinking.

I asked him if he would accept that, at this moment in his brain's lifecycle, it was okay to let his brain rest from the need to always be feeling great and passionate about his business?

I asked him if it was ok to do that?

He said, 'I've never looked at it in that way. I always thought that I had to be passionate about what I do all of the time, and that if I wasn't, there was something wrong with my business. Or worse still, something wrong with me!'

I didn't have to say much more than this - he got it.

He understood that high performers have highs and lows, but the key is to accept the low, not as a low, but as a rejuvenation phase, for the next burst in life.

He reported back to me a few months later, sharing with me that business and life couldn't be better. He even welcomed the low motivation days, because they were just his brain's way of saying, 'Take a break, buddy, you're trying way too hard.'

If I wake up and find myself lacking motivation, I don't fight it. I go through my routine and write down all of my urgent and important projects for the day in my Red Day® Book (my customised project planner).

I look at that plan and, if nothing about it excites me to get to work, I simply walk away from it.

My brain needs a rest. Remember your brain is an organ, just like your heart - it can't be working at its maximum pace all of the time.

The beauty of owning your own business is that you can call the shots with your own time. I go with the flow and end up doing some light 'low brain work', make social catch up calls, go for a walk along the seaside and indulge in a heavenly ice cream. They are all low-level brain activities.

You'll be amazed how, in no time at all, you will find yourself recharged and ready to get back to work.

Remember, the brain is an organ and all our organs need a break. I didn't say they need to stop, they just need some pampering now and then from being under constant loads.

Working longer hours is not a sign of strength - it is a sign of weakness and low confidence.

Taking quality Green Days™ and working smarter, with shorter, impactful hours is a sign of strength and high confidence

Anything can be tackled when you are in high confidence mode. Protect your confidence at all times. Rest when you need to rest.

Being able to break free from the 8th day of the week syndrome is a sign that your confidence is at its highest.

Lesson 18: We Crave What We Don't Have

'Social media is now your local neighbourhood multiplied by millions of other neighbours.'

At what age do we learn that bigger is better?

One.

That's right - from age one onwards parents and teachers, mostly unconsciously, are reinforcing the concept that 'bigger and more' is better.

Just take a closer look at a parent or teacher when they describe that something is big. They say things like, 'Wow, look how big that toy is.'

Now, look at their hand gestures, their facial expressions, the widening of their eyes and smile, and their vocal tone when they are saying that it's big.

Now take a closer look at the same parents and teachers when they refer to something small. This time they say things like, 'Aw, look at how small that toy is.' They automatically shrink down their hand movements, their body size, even their eyes, mouths and shoulders. Their vocal tone gets smaller too - it comes across as 'poor thing'.

That's a pretty powerful image being stamped into a kid's brain from a very early age. And it sticks for life.

One of the consequences of that powerful conditioning is our drive to 'keep up with the Joneses'. Bigger and more is better, right?

So what do young kids, teenagers and young adults all want? They want MORE.

They want BIGGER.

And sometimes they want MORE AND BIGGER.

That said, if you're into body image and you happen to be large, well, then the opposite is true: Less and Smaller is perceived as better. Either way, it's craving what you don't have,

Marketers love this. They love that it doesn't take much to tap into this deeply engrained, conditioned behaviour.

We are cleverly bombarded with marketing messages that remind us just how much more the 'Joneses' have than us.

Everyday, in my street mailbox, I receive a bundle of catalogues that show me all the things I am missing out on. I turn on the TV and I see what I don't have. I turn on the radio and these same messages are reinforced. I browse the internet and the same messages are there too - the only difference is that I can click the 'close' box and make those annoying little pop-ups disappear. Yes, they disappear, but once seen, even for a microsecond, my brain has captured what I don't have, whether I like it or not.

Sometimes, however, I like the 'keeping up with the Joneses' mentality.

It's not all bad.

I've noticed that, when I have a major clean up of my gardens, the following week one or two of the other neighbours get inspired and have their gardens all cleaned up too - it can be a good trigger. Gardens that have a trim always end up looking younger, fresher and more lively. It's beautiful.

But - and it's a big but -

I've consulted with enough businesses, families and individuals over the last twenty years to share with you that craving what you don't have is one of the biggest drivers for those who end up working the 8th day of the week.

Popular social media sites don't reflect the reality of people's lives, they just reflect the version they want you to see.

If you want to know what you are missing out on in life, just check out your friends on all of the different social media sites. They will show you the gaps you have in your life.

They will show you in an 'instant' what your friends or friends of friends are doing, what they are wearing, where they are travelling, who they are hanging out with, and what they just bought, sold and invested in. You'll see it all in an instant and, to top it off, they'll even have words of envy attached to make you really want to go out into the world and achieve more. Right?

Wrong!

Don't misunderstand me, there is a time and place for all of the different social mediums out there.

They can inspire and connect you… but they can also depress and disconnect you, deceiving you into thinking that you don't have enough or, worse still, that you are not enough of a person to deserve what others have.

Social media is now your local neighbourhood multiplied by millions of other neighbourhoods.

Keeping up with the Joneses is no longer confined to your

immediate family and neighbours. The whole world is now seen as your neighbourhood - the Joneses are everywhere!

Don't be fooled.

Your friends and your friends' friends are only posting up snippets of their lives.

We get to see the best parts of their lives.

We then believe that the snippet is the whole picture. It really isn't.

The story behind the snippet tells a very different tale.

It is not uncommon to see an envious picture of someone one week and then to find out in the following week that they have tried to take their life.

It's shocking - it's an extreme example, but it is a real one and it will keep on happening.

Research is now showing that people who use social media to keep in touch are becoming increasingly depressed. They believe that they have less.

Maybe the grass is greener on the other side BUT the weeds are the same!

You have everything you need - everything else is wants. And while it's healthy to want, make sure you don't have to work 8 days a week for a false picture.

Get out of the 8th day of the week syndrome and be real with yourself.

Lesson 19: When You Play More Golf, You'll Have A Better Business!

'Find or rediscover an activity that is 100% unrelated to your business.'

I know from experience that to an 8th day of the weeker this lesson sounds ridiculous.

How can you play more golf and expect to have a better business?

Well, you will have to or you will go out of business!

Working less is a great incentive for becoming more creative and effective with the little time you have left. You become smarter at what you take on and what you don't take on, instead of trying to take on everything.

I have enjoyed a long weekend off every weekend for the last 728 weeks of my life. That's 14 years' worth of 'mini-retirements' and going strong.

But it wasn't always like that.

There was a time when my days and nights were devoured by business and how to make it better. It was an around the clock addiction. I only ever talked business. Business thinking and doing consumed me.

So I can appreciate the scepticism when an 8th day of the weeker doubts that it is possible to reduce your working hours and increase your business results at the same time. It goes against the grain of everything we've been taught.

For a business owner, I play a lot of golf - more than most retirees do - and I still manage to do a lot of business by working no more than 24 hours a week and taking at least 170 days off a year.

I love my business, because it allows me to play a lot of golf.

I love my golf, because it allows me to do a lot of business.

So how does this work? What's the secret to working less and achieving more?

It's surprisingly simple - as most good things are.

Go out and find, or rediscover, an activity that is 100% unrelated to your business.

For me it was golf.

I absolutely love golfing, so the golf strategy works extremely well for me.

For you it may be something else entirely. It may be playing an instrument, taking up a hobby, a sport, painting, gardening, travel, camping. Maybe its something you did when you were younger. Whatever it is, find that 'something' that you love to do.

Here's why it's so important to your success:

Doing too much of one thing burns out your creativity and you become stale. If all you focus on is business, day in day out, you will end up losing your ability to think outside of the box.

Now, if I procrastinate, muck around or get distracted with '10-cent' activities, it would mean I have to call up my golfing buddies and cancel my game with them. I'm not prepared to do that, because I love my golf, and so I'm not prepared to procrastinate in my business either.

Now that's a huge incentive for me to stay on task and focus on getting all of my urgent and important high level activities done and dusted before a golf day comes around.

If I didn't have golf as something else to look forward to, I would have easily spread my four days of work into the fifth day and most likely into the sixth and seventh day.

People are too busy working to take time away from working.

They fear letting go of their control over their business. They fear that, if they are not there, things won't get done properly or they will miss out on sales.

'Good', I say! Miss out on sales. Let things go wrong. How else will you know what needs to be fixed in your business? How else will it start to work without you being there every day?

Get right away from your business, go play your 'golf' equivalent, and let things happen in your business. Then, with a fresh mind, go back into your business and create system solutions to all of the problems that occurred while you were away doing your thing. Play more golf and you'll have a better business. Makes sense now?

Why work your guts out all of your life so you can retire? Retire now. Retire every week for three days. This way you will never have to retire from work.

And yes, I am implying that you should work forever!

Why?

Our brains need to work, they need stimulation (not high stress, but stimulation). We need to do things to keep us fit and healthy, so never stop working. Always have projects of some type on the go.

Projects don't have to be money related. There are social projects, holiday projects, charity projects, sporting projects, mentoring projects... even grandkids are projects.

We are designed to always be doing something - sleeping, eating, moving, thinking - and they all involve brainwork.

When you stop using your body muscles they shrink and wither away like salad leaves that have been in the fridge way past their expiry date. Our brains are no different.

The idea of retirement is stupid and idiotic. It makes you a baby again - dependant and useless.

My Green Days™ are my mini-retirement days, days that are 100% no business. These days are essential to boosting my passion and creativity for my business.

I take Green Days™, not because I don't love what I do, but because I love what I do. And I want to continually love it each and every week of my life. And the best way I know how to sustain that love for my business is to avoid burning out.

A client of mine was running a removals business and he used this lesson to test how 'fit' his business was without him.

He figured that the busiest day of the working week for him was a Friday. Most people wanted to move and be in their new home on a Friday.

So what did he do?

He took Friday off as his Green Day™.

He told me that if there were any weaknesses in his business they would show up on a Friday, when his business was most under stress, both people and system wise. And he was spot on. For the next 12 weeks he took Fridays off and was constantly bombarded with problems that needed his attention.

But guess what? After 4 months of pursuing this lesson he was completely free to take all Fridays off and have a mini-retirement each and every week!

The lesson made him sit back and address all of the things that the business needed to systemise so it could become more effective and no longer rely on his day-to-day presence and input.

His business was now Green Day™ fit.

With the right, simple systems in place, the team took over 80% of what he used to - things he thought nobody else could do as well as him.

The systems he and his team put in place allowed him to take a mini-retirement each week. He was more creative with his ability to solve cashflow issues, customer and employee issues and as a result he ended up selling his business for 12 times what he bought it for.

Reverse your thinking: Instead of increasing your working week, reduce your working week by one day and ask yourself, 'What has to be done in order for my business to produce the same amount of profits without me being there for that one day?'

The goal is not to have a business that works without you (it will always need you to lead it), but to create a business that frees you up to take on bigger opportunities. And that's the role of a business owner – YOU.

Lesson 20: Your Business Is An Illusion
The Final Lesson (Until We Meet Again)

*'How your customers/clients view
your business is also an illusion.'*

Your business is a 'Blivet'.

This is an example of a Blivet:

A Blivet is an impossible object,
an illusion.

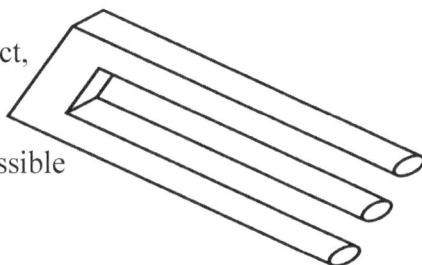

Your business is also an impossible
object, an illusion!

Why?

Grab someone close to you right now and ask him or her how
many prongs do they see in the above object.

Some will say, 'Three'. Some will say, 'Two'. And some will say,
'This is messing with my brain. I don't know!' or words to that
effect.

So who is right?

There is no right and no wrong - it's an impossible object after all.
It's all a matter of perception. It depends on your point of view.

Most business owners are blinded by a point of view that works
against them. They suffer from 'Blivet' thinking - a mental illusion
about how their business should operate and it's making them work
crazy long hours for little return.

Before you complete this book, I need to show you both the power and the destruction that Blivet thinking has on your businesses progress and success.

Here is what **destructive** and **constructive** Blivet thinking might sound like in your business:

Perception: 'I don't have all of the facts to be able to put this product on the market.'
Destructive Blivet Response: 'Lets put the product on hold until we have all of the facts.'
Consequences: The service/product gets put on hold and sometimes never sees the light of day, your business stagnates in limbo, and the people involved in the project also stagnate. You work harder and longer hours trying to come up with the ideal solution.

Now for the opposite approach in thinking:

Constructive Blivet Response: 'I have enough information to release it to the marketplace. We'll tweak things along the way based on how the marketplace reacts.'
Consequences: The release of your service or product produces excitement amongst your employees and it's customers. There's unforeseen 'magic' in getting a project started. Things happen that you would never have expected.

You get to solve a problem for the customer. Your willingness to monitor how the service/product is perceived allows you the opportunity to further innovate a better service/product along the way. It will inspire other products and services as a result.

Dramatically different thinking produces dramatically different results.

How you look at your business is an illusion. How your

customers/clients view your business is also an illusion.

Knowing this: there is no failure, only progress.

Here are my most powerful ways for you to progress in both your business and personal life by adopting the following constructive Blivet thinking strategies:

1/ Become A 20% Action Person.

That's right, 20%.

The idea of aiming for 100% is destructive Blivet thinking. It was most likely injected into us in our early school years. We were in awe and jealous of those who could get 100% correct in an exam.

Business is not about 100%.

The idea that 100% is the benchmark is very destructive for business owners. It's where the idea of perfectionism comes from and, along with it, inferiority complexes of not being good enough.

Don't buy into it. It's all an illusion. And this is how to make it work for you, not against you:

**Whenever you start or get stuck on a project become a
20% Action – 80% Results Person.**

Ask yourself this one key question:

**'What's the 20% Action I can take right now
that will give me an 80% Result in my first step?'**

The reason I have my clients ask this disarmingly powerful question is that I know 20% of your actions will give you 80% of the result you're looking for.

2/ Limit the time it takes for you to take that first 20% Action step.

How long you take to do something is determined by how long you give yourself to do it.

The less time you have to decide, the faster you'll take action, and when you're focused on just taking the first 20% action step, it should almost be an instant action.

Imagine how much more you would achieve in your business if you adopted this strategy?

3/ Become An 80% Results Person:

100% Results thinking puts way too much pressure on your ability to think clearly. 100% Results thinking carries with it an undercurrent of the fear, 'What if it's not 100% right?' This fear stops us from progressing and from being happily creative. It's a game stopper.

The biggest reason to become an 80% Results person is that your 80% Results may be perceived as a 100% result by others!

So what are you stressing about?
Here's a practical way of understanding all of this:

Take a look at the clothes in your wardrobe.

When you got dressed today, you had many options.

Lets say the 'project' was to choose clothes that will make you look and feel good for a meeting today.

You have many ways of dressing for this occasion, just as you have many ways of tackling any given business problem.

So what's the solution for doing this project fast and with an 80% Result?

(Keep in mind that you probably wear 20% of your clothes 80% of the time.)

Take the first 20% Action: take out the items you know you look good in and are comfortable wearing (this eliminates 80% of the other options)

This 20% Action will give you 80% of the Result you are looking for. Now, move on to the next 20% Action in the next part of your project - putting on the right shoes!

If I only gave you 2 minutes to complete this project, would it have been almost as good as if you were given 2 hours instead?

Most likely, yes, and you would have freed yourself up by 1 hour and 58 minutes to be able to progress other, more valuable, projects.

Become a 20% Action – 80% Result person for one week and see what happens to your businesses progress and your free time. You won't know yourself.

Apply it in your personal life. Try it out on your important relationships.

If you have employees, teach them to adopt the same strategy in their role in the business.

Remember, you're paying for the 1 hour and 58 minutes that is totally unnecessary when you could have achieved an 80% Result in 2 minutes. That's a huge saving of your time and money and that saving is better invested in doing other, more valuable, work.

Break free from The 8th Day Of The Week today.

Apply 20% of the lessons in this book with an 80% Result mindset and you will be free to create and enjoy not only a bigger bank balance, but more importantly a bigger balance in all areas of your life.

Congratulations and thank you for travelling this journey with me.

Reward yourself. Go and do something you don't normally do, with someone you love. Share these lessons with them. Show them that you are ready for a new beginning and you are ready to take them with you on that journey.

Here's to you, your courage and your future.

George Bakmchev